THE CONQUEST OF SUFFERING

THE CONQUEST OF SUFFERING

An enlarged Anthology of George Grimm's Work on Buddhist Philosophy and Metaphysics

P.J.SAHER

MLBD PUBLICATIONS

Motilal Banarsidass Publications

MOTILAL BANARSIDASS
PUBLICATIONS
4741/23, Ansari Road, Daryaganj, New Delhi - 110002 (India)
Email: *mlbd@mlbd.com* | *sales@mlbd.com* | *exports@mlbd.com*
Website: *www.mlbd.com*

The Conquest of suffering
by
P.J. Saher

2nd Reprint Edition: Delhi, 2022
First Edition: Delhi, 1977

Published in India by Motilal Banarsidass Publications

ISBN : 978-93-91759-76-6 (PB)

Printed and bound in India

DEDICATED TO

the Buddhist University

of

Sri Lanka

(Ceylon)

May the glory of

Anuradhapura and Kataragama

shine again—namo Buddhāya !

FOREWORD

Today the value of the individual has, more radically than at any other time in history, been called in question by technology and all that it entails. We have become strangers in the environment we ourselves created. There is a disquieting increase in the number of people who feel they have failed in life, who "drop out", "break down" and who, consciously or not, escape from the heavy burden of responsibility towards family, society and themselves. These panic actions are no long term solution to the problems which we have to face today. No lethargic passivism, nostalgic escapism or presumptious social revolutionism can evoke that fundamental change which has become a pressing need. There seems to be but one way to come out of the present crisis unscathed : through an absolute effort on the part of each individual to restore his inner order and harmony and to come to terms with his essential nature. The change which is demanded from us today is, in the last analysis, nothing short of a complete transformation of consciousness, of the human personality as such. The cultural and historical arguments for this assumption have, among others, been supplied by Professor Jean Gebser.

The question of why and how human personality should be changed has for long occupied the Eastern mind, and it has been analysed with uncompromising accuracy and dispassionate logic by the enlightened sage Gautama Siddhārtha. The Buddha's singularity lies in his emphatic insistence on first-hand knowledge. Rejecting the shaky reasoning and a priori theorising of contemporary philosophy, he relied exclusively on experience. This decidedly positivistic approach was the great novum which the Buddha introduced to Indian metaphysical thought. He did away with all clever speculation, with tradition, mysticism and superstition and took as his only refuge personal experience of reality. He did this not because he wanted to create a new system, one of the favourite activities of the Indian mind, but merely to find a way to conquer his own inner insecurity, doubt and sorrow. In the course of his determined enquiry he realised four fundamental truths :—

1. Suffering is universal ; it appears in the form of pain, anxiety, frustration, grief, loss etc.
2. Suffering has a definite cause ; ignorance about the illusory nature of the ego.
3. Suffering can be terminated.
4. The way to terminate suffering is through the noble eightfold path : right view, right resolve, right speech, right action, right livelihood, right exertion, right mindfulness and right meditation.

These four points came to constitute the Magna Charta of all branches of Buddhism ; their central aim being the progressive dismantling of the I and the demonstration of its utter illusoriness. This does not result in a dull state of egolessness, as has so often been suggested, but leads to the freedom from the ego which is distinctly different.

These mal-identifications or superimpositions of a static I on the continuously changing stream of psychomental energies have their root in the unconscious. Hence the Buddha, long before psychoanalysis, stressed the importance of conquering the latent dispositions buried in the depths of our consciousness. Total freedom from the I, the termination of the eternal cycle of egotistic life, is possible only after these subliminal root-causes of suffering have been completely burnt out. The measure of success lies in the achievement of that indescribable state of freedom from the sway of suffering which the Buddha called *nirvāṇa.*

The Buddha does not ask for any belief or blind acceptance of his teaching. He, in full agreement with the modern scientific attitude, challenges us to experiment with his method and test his statements. He demands that we should be "refuges unto ourselves, lamps unto ourselves". For he also leaves no trace of doubt about the fact that suffering, its rise and termination, do not depend on any outer agent, but solely on each individual being. Thus it becomes plain that in this age the Buddha's teaching could prove essential in recovering and re-establishing the submerged individual and instrumental in man's quest for self-understanding.

This book is an unusually lucid and inspiring presentation of the Buddha's method and approach. It reflects, like the author's previous works, his deep concern for man as well as his knowledge and wisdom and that experience which only comes with the personal actualisation of the essence of all *philosophia perennis*.

Yoga Research Association
London

Georg Feuerstein

LIST OF ABBREVIATIONS

A	Aṣṭasāhasrikā Prajñāpāramita, ed. R. Mitra BI 1888, trsl. E. Conze, BI 1958.
AAA	Abhisamayālaṅkārāloka, by Haribhadra, ed. U. Wogihara, 1932-5.
Ad	Aṣṭādaśasāhasrikā Prajñāpāramitā.
AK	Abhidharmakośa, by Vasubandhu, = L. de la Vallée-Poussin. L'AK de Vasubandhu, trad, et annoté, 6 vols, 1923-31.
AKP	S. Schayer, Ausgewaehlte Kapitel aus der Prasannapadā, 1931.
AM	Asia Major.
AN	Aṅguttara Nikāya.
AO	Acta Orientalia.
AOKM	Akten des 24ten Internationalen Orientalisten-Kongresses München, 1959.
Asl	Atthasālinī, by Buddhaghosa (cy to DhS), ed. PTS 1897, trsl. as 'The Expositor' 2 vols., PTS 1920-1.
B	Buddhism, E. Conze, 1951.
BB	Bibliotheca Buddhica.
Bcv	Bodhicaryāvatāra, by Śāntideva.
Bcv-p	cy (pañjikā) to Bcv by Prajñākaramati, ed. BI 1901-5.
B.E.	Buddhist Era.
Beckh	H. Beckh, Buddhismus, 1928.
BI	Bibliotheca Indica.
BL	Buddhist Logic, Th. Stcherbatsky. 2 vols., BB 1932, 1930.
BM	Buddhist Meditation, E. Conze, 1956.
BS	Buddhist Scriptures, E. Conze, 1959.
BSOAS	Bulletin of the School of Oriental and African Studies.
BT	Buddhist Texts, ed. E. Conze, 1954.
Buston	Bu-ston, History of Buddhism, trsl. E. Obermiller, 2 vols., 1931-2.

BWB	Buddhist Wisdom Books, E. Conze, 1958.
Comp.	Compendium of Philosophy, by Z. Aung and C. A. F. Rhys Davids, 1910 (a trsl. of Anuruddha's Abhidammatta-saṅgaha).
CPD	Critical Pali Dictionary, 1924 *sq.*
cy	commentary
Da-Bhu.	Daśabhūmikasūtra, ed. J. Rahder, 1926.
Dhp	Dhammapada, ed. and trsl. S. Radhakrishnan, 1950.
DhS	Dhammasangani, ed. PTS 1885; trsl. A Buddhist Manual of Psychological Ethics, C.A.F. Rhys Davids, 1900.
Divy.	Divyāvadāna, ed, Cowell and Neil, 1886.
DN	Dīgha Nikāya.
Dutt	N. Dutt, Aspects of Mahāyāna Buddhism and its relation to the Hīnayāna, 1930.
EA	Etudes Asiatiques.
EB	Eastern Buddhist.
Edgerton	F. Edgerton, Buddhist hybrid Sanskrit grammar and dictionary, 1953.
Enc Bu	Encyclopedia of Buddhism, 1957.
Exp	The Expositor; see at Asl.
EZB	Essays in Zen Buddhism, D.T. Suzuki.
F	E. Frauwallner, Die Philosophie des Buddhismus, 1956.
Froebes	J. Froebes, Lehrbuch der experimentellen Psychologie, 1923.
GOS	Gaekwad Oriental Series.
Grimm	G. Grimm, The doctrine of the Buddha, 1958.
Har Dayal	The Bodhisattva doctrine in Buddhist Sanskrit literature, 1932.
HBI	Histoire du Bouddhisme Indien. E. Lamotte, I, 1958.
Heiler	F. Heiler, Die buddhistische Versenkung, 1922.
Henderson-Gillespie	Textbook of Psychiatry, 1936.
Hob.	Hōbōgirin, 4 fasc., 1929-37.
IC	Instant et Cause, L. Silburn, 1955.
IHQ	Indian Historical Quarterly.

IIJ	Indo-Iranian Journal.
JAs	Journal Asiatique.
JBRS	Journal of the Bihar Research Society.
JGIS	Journal of the Greater India Society.
JRAS	Journal of the Royal Asiatic Society.
Keith	A.B. Keith, Buddhist philosophy in India and Ceylon, 1923.
Kimura	R. Kimura, Historical study of the terms Hīnayāna and Mahāyāna, 1927.
KSP	Karmasiddhiprakaraṇa, trad. E.Lamotte as traité de l'acte de Vasubandhu, MCB iv 1936.
LalV	Lalita Vistara, ed. S. Lefmann, 1902-8; trad. Foucaux, 1884-92.
Leuba	J. H. Leuba, The Psychology of Religious Mysticism.
LS	Laṅkāvatāra Sūtra, ed. B. Nanjio 1923; trsl. D.T. Suzuki, 1932.
MCB	Mélanges Chinoises et Bouddhiques.
Mhvy	Mahāvyutpatti.
Mil	Milindapañha, ed. Trenckner, 1880; trsl. T.W. Rhys Davids, SBE, 1890-4.
MM	Manual of a Mystic, PTS 1916.
MMK	(Mūla) Madhyamakakārikā, ed. BB 4, 1903-13.
MN	Majjhima Nikāya.
Ms	Mahāyānasaṁgraha, trad. E. Lamotte, La somme du grand véhicule d'Asaṅga, 2 vols., 1938-9.
MSL	Mahāyānsūtrālaṁkāra. ed. S. Levi, 1907,
MT	Middle Treatise (Chung-lun), T. 1564.
Murti	T.R.V. Murti, The central philosophy of Buddhism, 1955.
Mv	Mahāvastu, ed. S. Senart, 3 vols., 1882-97. trsl. J.J. Jones, 3 vols, 1949-56.
M-v-t.	Madhyāntavibhāgaṭīkā. by Sthiramati, ed. S. Yamagucchi, 1934.
Nānamoli	The Path of Purification (=VM), trsl. Bhikkhu Nāṇamoli, 1956.
Nyanatiloka	Visuddhi-magga older der Weg zur Reinheit, uebs. Nyanatiloka. 1952.

OLZ	Orientalistische Literaturzeitung.
P	Pañcaviṁśatisāhasrikā Prajñāpāramitā, Bibl. in PL 42.
PDc	The Pali Text Society's Pali-English Dictionary
PhEW	Philosophy East and West.
PL	The Prajñāpāramitā Literature, E. Conze, 1960.
Pras.	Prasannapadā, by Candrakīrti, ed. BB 4, 1903-13.
Pts.	Paṭisambhidā-magga, ed. PTS, 2 vols., 1905, 1907.
PTS	Pali Text Society.
Pv-A	Petavatthu cy ed, PTS, 1894.
PW	The Large Sūtra on Perfect Wisdom, E. Conze, 1961.
Rahula	W. Rahula, What the Buddha taught, 1959.
Regamey	C. Regamey, Buddhistiche Philosophie, 1950 (Bibliography).
Rgv	Ratnagotravibhāga, ed. E.H. Johnston and T. Chowdhury, 1950.
RO	Rocznik Orientalistyczny.
Robinson	R.H. Robinson, Madhyamika Studies in Fifth-century China. London Thesis. 1959.
Ś	Śatasāhasrikā Prajñāpāramitā. Bibl. PL 37.
S	Sanskrit.
Sa	Saptaśatikā Prajñāpāramitā. Bibl. PL 62-3.
Saund.	Saundarananda-kāvya, by Aśvaghoṣa, ed. E.J. Johnston, 1928, trsl. Johnston, 1932,
SBE	Sacred Books of the East.
Śi	Śikṣāsamuccaya, by Śāntideva, ed. BB I 1897-1902. trsl. Bendall and Rouse, 1922.
Siddhi	La Siddhi, trad. et annotée par L.de la Vallée-Poussin, 2 vols. 1928-30.
SN	Saṁyutta Nikāya.
SOR	Serie Orientale Roma.
SP	Saddharmapuṇḍarīkasūtra, ed. U. Wogihara and C. Tsuchida, 1935.
SS	Selected Sayings from the Perfection of Wisdom, E. Conze, 1955.

Stace	W.T. Stace, The teachings of the mystics, 1960.
Sn	Suttanipāta, ed. Lord Chalmers, 1932.
Suv	Suvikrāntavikramiparipṛcchā, ed. R. Hikata, 1958.
Suzuki St.	D.T. Suzuki, Studies in the Laṅkāvatāra Sūtra, 1930.
SW	Der Satz vom Widerspruch, E. Conze, 1932.
T	Tibetan
TI	Taishō Issaikyō.
Takakasu	J. Takakusu, The essentials of Buddhist philosophy, 1947.
Th	Theragāthā, ed. PTS 1883.
TLS	Times Literary Supplement.
Traité	Le traité de la grande vertue de sagesse, E. Lamotte, 2 vols., 1944, 1949.
Tri	Triṃśikā by Vasubandhu, ed. S. Levi, 1925.
Ts	Tattvasaṁgraha, by Śāntirakshita with cy of Kamalaśīla, ed. GOS, 2 vols., 1926, trsl. GOS, 2 vols., 1937-9
Ud	Udāna PTS, 1902.
Ud-A	cy to Udāna.
V	Vajracchedikā ed. E. Conze, SOR 1957.
VM	Visuddhimagga, by Buddhaghosa; ed. C.A.F. Rhys Davids, 2 vols., PTS 1920-1 (quoted by pages); ed. H.C. Warren, 1950 (quoted by chapters and paragraphs).
Vv-A	cy to Vimānavatthu ed. PTS 1901.
Wolf	History of science in the seventeenth century.
Woodworth	Experimental Psychology.
WZKM	Wiener Zeitschrift zur Kunde des Morgenlandes.
WZKSO	Wiener Zeitschrift fur die Kunde Süd-und Ostasiens.
ZDMG	Zeitschrift der deutschen morgenlandischen Gesellschaft.
ZJC	Zen and Japanese Culture, D.T. Suzuki, 1959.

CONTENTS

CHAPTER I

TO BE OR NOT TO BE

> "Nothing will do us greater service in getting rid of suffering than a well-directed mind."
>
> *Buddha*

The problem of the annihilation of suffering coincides with the conquest of the ego through which the human being is linked to the world and thereby to suffering. In the measure in which I succeed in liberating myself from my ego, to that extent do I outgrow the world and its sufferings. Having wholly freed myself from the components of my personality, I regard it as something entirely alien to me, and I see the world and suffering in the same way. My personality, the world and suffering have nothing more to do with me, for I have withdrawn myself from them. I am still in the world, but I am no longer of the world. "....I have vanquished the world, and unspotted by the world I remain."[1]

Yet the man who has outgrown his ego, has by no means solved the problem of annihilating suffering. Were it merely a question of conquering the present ego, there would be no serious problem, as the ego dissolves in death. The important need is to prevent the new formation of the psyche in the moment of dissolution, since, at the moment of death, the psyche objectifies itself afresh.

The Buddha described how this presented itself to him on the peak of insight as the first and second of the three great Revelations that arose within on the night he reached Buddhahood:

"With thought thus fixed, cleansed, purged and stainless; clear of all dross, supple, serviceable, firm and unswerving, I turned my mind towards the recollection and recognition of

1. *Aṅguttara-Nikāya*, IV, 36

previous modes of existence." Having referred to his previous lives, he said: "This...was the first knowledge to which I attained, ignorance banished, knowledge gained; darkness dispelled, light won...."

He then directed his thought towards the perception of the disappearing and reappearing of beings. Those "....given to things evil in deeds, words and thoughts....at the dissolution of the body, after death, depart upon a sorry journey, downward to loss in the world of the hells." On the other hand, "....those given to good deeds, words and thoughts....earn a happy lot. At the breakup of the body, after death, they fare forth upon a happy journey and come to the heaven-world."

He then directed his mind to the "....perception of the destruction of influences. 'This is Suffering. Thus comes the Arising of Suffering. Thus comes the Cessation of Suffering. This is the Path that leads to the Cessation of Suffering. These are the Influences. Thus comes the arising of the Influences. Thus comes the Cessation of the Influences. This is the Path that leads to the Cessation of the Influences.'...Thus perceiving...., my mind was released from the Influences of Ignorance. 'I am delivered...Life is lived out, the holy goal achieved: done all that was to do; no more is this world for me."[1]

In direct vision the Buddha saw the endless chain of his bygone personalities, conditioned each time by a new birth. He also saw that all creatures are ever and again conducted from death to renewed birth in an incessant round. This boundless circle of rebirths, he described as "....a circle of unending despair."

How this incessantly renewed objectification of the ego was to be brought to an end once and for all, was for him the great question. Its solution was given to him by the third wisdom, of which he said : "Then I saw and knew: 'Assured am I of deliverance; this is my final birth; never more shall I return hither."[2]

The texts are full of passages which again and again point to this escape from the tormenting circle of rebirths as the sup-

1. *Majj. Nik.*, 36. Discourse
2. *Ibid.*, 26. Discourse

reme goal of all effort. "The saint who seeks peace bears his last body to the grave." And, more poetically:

"Through countless ages I have been devoted to the body:
This is the last of them,—this living conjunction.
The round of birth and death : there is now no more coming
to be of it."[2]

A man can only regard himself as finally freed from suffering, when he reaches the unshakeable conviction that he is not only something entirely different from the components of his present personality, and is therefore immune from its fate, but also that his present ego is the last to which he will be chained. In other words, that his coming death is his last and is the gateway through which he escapes for ever from the round of rebirths.

The Buddha explains the principal cause of this incessant and successive reproduction of individualities. He points out the conditions of this process in the famous formula of origination through dependence, *paticcasamuppāda.* The Perfected One is alienated from the five groups, out of which the complex called personality—which represents the world— is built up. He is cured of the delusion that they are in any way an efflux of his essence, and he is cured so completely that, even in contemplating them, the thought of his I does not arise in him. To him they are no more than processes which, basically, have nothing at all to do with him. From the unmoving pole of his real essence, which lies beyond them, he sees them as foreign elements rising incessantly from the realm of the uncognizable, or from No-thing-ness.

The Buddha defined personality as made up of the five groups of grasping. These are : "...the grasping-group of the corporeal form, the grasping-group of sensation, the grasping-group of perception, the grasping-group of the activities of the mind, the grasping-group of cognition."[3]

Thus personality consists of the body, the sensations, the perceptions, the activities of the mind, and cognition. These are more than groups. They are *groups of grasping*, and they

1. *Aṅgut. Nik.*. IV, 16
2. *Theragāthā*, V. 258, 259
3. *Majj. Nik.*, 44. Discourse

constitute the ego. According to the Buddha, our essence is not contained in our personality. We grasp our personality so tightly that we imagine ourselves to consist in it.

The ego, or personality, consists of these five groups. The material body provides the basis of the personality. It originates in the moment of conception from the chemical materials the Buddha sums up under the four chief elements, earth, water, fire and air. These make up the female egg and the male spermatic cell. They also furnish the matter for building up the body. Formed by these elements, it is, throughout life, sustained by them.

This body, "endowed with the six organs of sense", is designated as the corporeal form, *rūpa*. The basis of personality —the body together with the sense organs—is only a collection of matter from external nature. Thus, for the Buddha, personality is mere conjunction of the substances comprised in the four chief elements. And on this fact he laid considerable stress. He pointedly and in great detail balanced the materials building up the body with those of the external world. He went further. He identified the former with the latter.

The body and the six organs of sense only form the basis of personality. But for personality to arise there must be the four further groups of sensation, perception, activities of the mind and cognition. This happens when the sense-organs pursue their own peculiar activities, each one intercepting and gathering a definite quality of the external world. Thus the eye gathers forms, the ears sounds, the nose odours, and so on.

Having listed the five senses of sight, hearing, smell, taste and touch, the Buddha said, "Do not these senses have a central point (*pāṭisaraṇa*), and does not something share in their domain and sphere action?"—"The five senses have *thinking* as a central point (*mana*), and thinking shares in their domain and sphere of action."[1] It is from the interlocking of a sense organ and the object of that sense that a content of consciousness arises. The Buddha said:

"If the organ of vision exists intact, but external forms do not come within its range and hence the proper interlocking is lacking, then the corresponding parcel of consciousness

1. *Majj. Nik.*, 43 Discourse

does not arise. And if outward forms do come within the reach of the organ of vision, but the appropriate interlocking fails to take place, then the corresponding parcel of consciousness does not arise."

If, for example, a man absent-mindedly looks upon a scene, he will not see the forms before him, and no consciousness of them will arise within him.

The fundamental insight consists in realising that all cognition is directed outwards. Accordingly the Essential and its whole domain are unattainable to it. If this standpoint is grasped, it is clear that the processes which yield the total impression of personality and world, are conditioned each by the other.

One arises through the other. The formula of origination through inter-dependence must be taken quite *impersonally*. This is due to the fact that, in the realm of the cognizable, a SELF is not to be found, while the realm of the uncognizable, precisely as such, yields no ideas at all. In fact, the formula of origination through inter-dependence, shows nothing more than mere processes running their course against the background of no thing, as the domain of our innermost essence, withdrawn from cognition, arising out of this "nothing" and always again disappearing into it :

"But who, O Lord, touches ?"

"The question is not rightly put,' the Exalted One replied. But if someone should ask me, 'On what, O Lord, depends touch ?' then this question would be put rightly, and the right answer would run thus : 'In dependence upon the six organs of sense arises touch, and in dependence upon touch arises sensation."

"But who, O Lord, feels ?"

"Neither is this question rightly put. I do not say, 'He feels.' But if someone should ask me, 'On what depends sensation ?' then this question would be rightly put, and the right answer to it would be : 'In dependence upon touch arises sensation."[1]

Because there is no permanent ego, room is left for a causal connection as conceived by the Buddha. If there were a perma-

1. *Saṁyutta Nikāya*, XII, 12

nent ego, then every question as to the primary causes of sensations and perceptions would be meaningless, and every causal connection as conceived by the Buddha impossible. No room would be left for any further cause. Equally, any deliverance from sensation and perception, and so from suffering, would be impossible. For it is impossible for a man to annihilate his real self.

Thus Saṁsāra is an endless chain of single personalities linked one to the other. Personality consists in the interworking of the five groups of grasping in such a manner that the corporeal organism—the first group—represents the personality's substratum—the six-senses-machine. This by means of the action of the organs of sense first rouses consciousness and then, in union with it, generates sensation, perception and the activities of the mind.

Since these five groups constitute all the elements and thereby the totality of all suffering, the corporeal organism might also most aptly be called *the machine of suffering*.

If the endless chain of misery that is called *Saṁsāra* is to be shown as being causally conditioned, then the corporeal organism, the machine itself, not only suffers but is the immediate cause of suffering. The corporeal organism receives its essence as a machine of suffering because it ages and withers, wears out, becomes grey, wrinkled and spent until, at last, it succumbs to complete ruin and dissolution in death. These inescapable qualities of the body—decline, decay and death—give to the whole process of personality and to life in all its details and in every direction the grim stamp of transiency. In doing so, they make life brim with suffering. Suffering culminates in old age and death. They are suffering's most pregnant expression. Because of this, the first question that presented itself to the Buddha was: "Are old age and death dependent on something?" To which he replied: "In dependence on birth arise old age and death."[1]

Old age and death are the culmination of a natural process, which begins with conception, proceeds to birth, a period of development, maturity, decline to decrepitude and, finally,

1. *Dīgha Nikāya*, XV

death itself. All these changes are conditioned by the same process whereby the organism itself arises with the accession of the element of consciousness.

Also to the organ of thinking an object must correspond. The objects of the organ of thinking are the objects of the other five senses. The Buddha describes the process as follows:

> "Through the eye and forms consciousness arises—visual consciousness. Through the ears and sounds consciousness arises—auditory consciousness. Through the nose and smells consciousness arises—olfactory consciousness. Through the tongue and flavours consciousness arises—gustatory consciousness. Through the body and tactile objects consciousness arises—tactile consciousness. Through the organ of thought and ideas consciousness arises—mental consciousness."[1]

This exposition yields an important result. Cognition is nothing at all substantial. It is simply the effect of a fixed conditioning cause. It is the interlocking of one of the activities of the six senses and its objects. It is present only as long as the cause exists, and it vanishes into nothing as soon as the cause disappears. It flares up the moment an organ of sense is excited through some appropriate external object. And it disappears if the organs of sense are put out of action. If I do not see, then there is no visual-consciousness. If I do not hear, there is no auditory -consciousness. And if all activities of the senses, including thinking, cease, then there is no consciousness at all. Apart from a conditioning cause there can be no condition. In short, cognition is something causally conditioned.

There must be contact with external objects before there can be consciousness. Before contact is established, and hence before consciousness is kindled in which I am first *touched* by the object appearing in it, this external object stimulating the sense-activity, and indeed even my own body certainly do not exist for me. Only in consequence of the kindling of consciousness am I *touched* by the external object to the extent that I am affected in the first instance by a *sensation*.

A sensation may be pleasant or unpleasant or neutral,

1. *Majj. Nik.*, 38. Discourse

but more than this cannot be experienced through sensation alone. At this stage, the object evoking the sensation is unknown. The object is recognized through perception which is directly attached to the sensation.

The Buddha saw that old age and death were inherent within the physical essence of the living creature. He saw that old age and death were masters of the body he occupied and he could not escape from them. He could only accept them with a calm and indifferent submission. As he said, "With patience I wear out my body."[1] On the other hand, there was the possibility of protecting himself in his inscrutable essence against a repetition of these processes, provided he could prevent a further new birth.

He thus found himself confronted with a new and unheard of problem. He needed to learn how, through the act of conception in the maternal womb, ever and again a new body endowed with senses is formed, with the result that, in the same act, consciousness comes down into it.

Only if he could solve this problem would it be at all possible to determine if the conditions of the act of birth—in the sense used by the Buddha—were such as it might be in human power to permit or prohibit. The Buddha solved this problem, and at the same time discovered the share we ourselves have in our conception. Thus he discovered the truth that everyone is in a position to decide whether or not he shall be reborn. It is precisely this power of making a future rebirth impossible, together with the absolute certainty of having succeeded in doing so, that deliverance is acquired and holiness gained. For he alone has escaped the circle of rebirths, forever passed beyond suffering, and thus become wholly delivered and perfectly sanctified, who can say of himself, "Rebirth is exhausted, lived out the holy life, done what was to do; no more is this world for me."[2] Or, as he said elsewhere, "Unshakeable is my deliverance, *this is the last birth,* I have nothing in common with this order of things."[3]

The only moment when it is possible to depart out of

1. *Theragāthā* V. 1002
2. *Sam. Nik.* XXXV. 28
3. *Majj. Nik.*, 28. Discourse

Saṁsāra is the moment a new birth takes place. That is, at the moment of death that is immediately followed by the new birth.

The solution of the riddle as to how the ego comes to be reborn again and again proved to be remarkably simple.

The Buddha sought to comprehend the process of becoming born as an integral part of another, larger process. If he discovered the conditions of the latter, then those of the former would become clear of themselves. The larger—which is the universal—process he found to be Becoming (*bhava*). Becoming is the only process within the world. There is no real being which has permanence. Everything is in a state of constant flux. Everything is nothing but *Becoming*. In the same way, everything living *becomes* in every possible world. It does this in the world of desires, in the world of forms and in the formless world.

Inorganic matter can never support the process of consciousness, which consists in sensation, perception and thought. The matter must be made *organic*. It must be *organized*. This is achieved by matter in the maternal womb building up into a corporeal form of a certain kind. In the womb, from the very beginning, the material body, including the organs of sense, are *organized*.

That is, they are made capable of serving as organs of sense. They assume a mysterious capacity entirely foreign to their essence. This is their capacity of causing consciousness to flame up as soon as they become active. Thus they engender sensation and perception. This transmutation of inorganic matter into organic, is equivalent to the transmutation of dead matter into living matter, for the latter expression denotes the capacity of arousing sensation. Vitality is completely bound up with the material body, and must totally disappear on the disintegration of such a body.

The machine of the six senses consists of the body endowed with vitality, and the five senses are nothing but manifestations of vitality. The Buddha expressed this fact by using the term *nāma-rūpa* for the six-senses-machine or the corporeal organism. By *rūpa* he meant the body consisting of inorganic matter, and by *nāma* the faculty of sensation, of perception, of thought, of contact, of attention and so on. As the *faculties* comprised under *nāma* form the kernel of what is called life, the meaning of *nāma-rūpa* is also that of a body capable of life.

Moreover, it may also be translated as mind-body, since the faculties comprised under *nāma* are the mental ones, called collectively the "mind". The sixth sense, the sense of thought, is not mentioned here, obviously because SĀRIPUTTA has just explained that it is the centre of the other senses, their "mainstay", and therefore must exist under the same fundamental antecedent condition as they do.

As a rule, only the faculty of *sensation* is given as the characteristic quality of life. This is certainly correct, as perception, thought, attention, etc., are simply the necessary consequences of sensation in the higher grades of life. Life, indeed, might be defined simply as the capacity of sensation.

The individual life is dependent on Becoming. As the Buddha said, "....birth arises in dependence on Becoming. Were there no Becoming at all of anything and in any sense, then birth would not occur. Thus the cause, origin, arising and dependence of birth is Becoming."

For the Buddha the problem of birth led to the further question: What is the sufficient cause of this unresting, unceasing Becoming in which we find ourselves involved? He gave his answer in the word *grasping*. A young man who has to choose his life's profession *grasps* the thought arising within him of becoming a merchant, an officer or an artist. He cultivates the thought, with the result that it is translated into action. *Becoming* sets in and progresses until the young man has actually *become* a merchant, an officer or an artist. In consequence of this grasping he has become that which he grasped. So it is with everyone all the time. As soon as some kind of grasping arises in the individual, *Becoming* begins. Always and everywhere we *become* that which we grasp, and we do so by identifying ourselves with that which becomes in consequence of the grasping. Even the body only *becomes* as long as the individual grasps food. If there is no *grasping* of food, the body ceases to become. It decays and dissolves.

Clearly, if I grasp nothing more, then nothing more can become in relation to me. Without grasping there can be no more becoming. As the Buddha said, "In dependence upon Grasping arises Becoming."

This line of reasoning is strange and unfamiliar to those steeped in western scientific thought. Our natural science regards all Becoming as due to nothing more than the incessant changes in matter caused by the laws dominating it. This matter and its laws are the only things given. Therefore everything in the universe, including man, in his attempts to understand man is limited to the exploration of nature, in which man is merely one genus among many others. Because of this it is only the *external* causal connection of phenomena that is recognized, while the innermost principle from which they take their origin are either overlooked or ignored. It leaves unexplained a basic residue. And we do not know how to behave when we suddenly find ourselves planted in the middle of the explanation of this, which is the very force of nature itself. For it is nothing less than this explanation which is presented to us in the intuition that *all Becoming proceeds from Grasping*.

The Buddha distinguished between *nāmakāya* and *rūpakāya*, the mental and material bodies. He explained that, were the mental body not there, then the material body would not be attainable by us, and so could not exist.

And if the material body did not exist, then those modes in which the mental body manifests itself; that is, by sensation, perception and mentation, would be impossible. Only by the conjunction of these two 'bodies' is the possibility of contact and, by contact, of sensation and mentation given. "Therefore, just this is the ground, the basis, the genesis, the cause of contact, to wit, *nāma-rūpa*."

Thus, according to the Buddha, the six-sense-machine—nāma-rūpa consists of two co-ordinate components which only in their conjunction yield the capacity of engendering consciousness and thereby sensation, perception and cognition. These are the material and mental bodies. How this spiritual and this material body is related we do not know. No more than we know how magnetism is related to steel. Nor does the Buddha tell us. But we must not take the rendering of *nāmakīya*—"mental body"—as signifying a substance indestructible and immaterial which inhabits the material body. By "mental body"nothing is designated but that unknown factor which transfers the material body into that state in which it is able to produce sensations, perceptions and cognition. In the doctrine of the Buddha the contrast of mind and matter, as understood by Christian theologians, does not exist. For him, mind and matter are not completely distinct.

They hold place in one and the same scale, matter being at the same time something coarsely mental; mind and soul at the same time being something subtly material.

This conception of the Buddha is in perfect harmony with modern physiology, for which the so-called mental or spiritual processes must ultimately be nothing but material processes of the most subtle kind. We may define the relation of the mental or spiritual body to the material one as the spiritual body representing a more intimate determinant. That is to say, a quality of the material body, in the same way that magnetism constitutes a quality of iron.

It results from this that vitality and the animal heat of the material body mutually condition each other. Vitality exists by reason of heat, and heat exists by reason of vitality.

Grasping is the energetical principle resident in all the separate phenomena of nature. It constitutes the essence of all natural forces. *The primary thing is not nature, not the world with its laws. The primary thing is the individual.*

Thus the problem consists in understanding how the Self, in its inscrutable essence, came into the world, or how it got into this realm of *Becoming*. Thus, for the Buddha, the problem is not how Becoming in itself, independent of the Self, is to be explained. It is from the outset and always, what is the ultimate and sufficient cause of the private individual? This means that the answer can never be found by external investigation, even if we search the entire universe. The answer can only be found by retiring from the world back into ourselves, to the "centre of our vital birth" and, by persistent introspection, seek to find out how we have come into all this Becoming in which we find ourselves so unhappily enmeshed.

According to the Buddha, whatever *becomes* about and for me, does so through an antecedent grasping that has arisen within me. In fact, it is precisely through this that I, myself, first became an individual. Due to this same type of grasping, every other individual comes into being. Every individual exists, not because of the laws of nature, but because, initially, there was *a taking hold* of life.

The Buddha does not teach expressly that all Becoming in the vegetable kingdom and in the domain of inorganic matter is conditioned by grasping. Not because this is wrong, but because here as everywhere, with unequalled logical consequence, he holds to his principle of dealing with nothing that does not serve to establish a truly holy life. He gives no attention to anything which merely satisfies a lust for knowledge. Becoming in the vegetable and inorganic kingdoms concerns us no further, as we can never slip back again into these domains. Nevertheless, the Buddha assumes as self-evident that existence in these domains consists in some kind of *grasping*.

Grasping, it is obvious, does not arise without cause. It is, indeed, causally conditioned. And the Buddha, with typical penetration and insight, saw exactly upon what grasping depended. He said : "In dependence upon *thirst* arises grasping." He used the term 'thirst' in the sense of 'longing' or 'desire'. "Suppose," he said, "there existed no thirst for anything, no thirst for forms, for sounds, for odours, for taste, for objects of touch, for ideas—if thirst were completely annihilated—there would then be no kind of grasping. Here then is the cause, origin, arising, dependence of grasping—namely, thirst."

This thirst, *taṇhā*, which relates to every kind of desire or craving for anything whatever in the world, is summed up in the objects of the six senses. And it comprises within itself conscious as well as unconscious volition.

"With his mind thus concentrated, made completely pure, utterly clear, devoid of depravity, free from dirty spots, ready to act, firm and imperturbable, he applies and directs it to the calling up of the mental body. He calls up from this body another body, having form, made of thought-stuff, having all limbs and parts, not deprived of any organ. . . ."[1]

The result is that the six-sense-machine—nāmə-rūpə—consists of two components. *Rūpa*, the body built up from

1. *Digha-Nik.* 11

materials of the outer world, is the supporter of the other component, namely vitality, called also *nāma* or *nāmakāya*, mental body. The latter constitutes a *quality* of the material body, in the same way that magnetism constitutes a quality of iron. As magnetism makes iron magnetic, vitality renders the material body organic. That is, it changes inorganic matter into organic matter.

Only the latter, in the form of a corporeal organism, is *capable* of arousing consciousness and thereby of bringing about contact with the outer world. As the Buddha said, "..both are inextricably connected; only as a unity may they come into existence."

From these expositions results the insight that eye-consciousness, ear-consciousness, etc., do not arise in the brain, as is inferred from the fact that, if a nerve leading from an organ of sense to the brain is severed, nothing more is seen or heard, etc. Eye-consciousness, ear-consciousness, etc., arise immediately in the eye, the ear, etc. The severing of the nerve merely interrupts contact with the source of the current, so that the nerve, so to speak, is no longer charged with vitality.

Thus the bodily organism as the six-sense-machine and as the substratum of personality, is fully comprehended. But the personality has the further substratum of consciousness. For the possibility of coming into contact with the world depends not only on the bodily organism, but also on this organism arousing consciousness in its sixfold sensual activity. Personality is, in fact, the homogeneous result of the bodily organism and the element of consciousness.

Cognition becomes active only through the interlocking of an individual organ of sense with an object in the outer world corresponding to it. Cognitive consciousness is conditioned by the corporeal organism, being a product of it. Conversely, the existence of the corporeal organism itself is conditioned by cognitive consciousness. If the corporeal organism did not enable cognitive consciousness, there would be no sensation.

But all sentient existence is dependent on grasping. Birth, as a part of the first stage of Becoming, has the same fundamental cause-*grasping*. And all grasping is rooted in thirst, in willing. Thus the search for the cause of our ever repeated rebirth led the Buddha to the discovery of the fundamental cause of all Becoming, that is of all being.

Our true essence lies beyond our personality and its components, even beyond the world. But we do not allow ourselves to be satisfied with it. We thirst for something else, for things entirely alien to our innermost essence, namely for the world of forms, sounds, odours, for a huge variety of tangible things, and also for intangible things such as power, authority and honour. And so great is our thirst for the world of forms, sounds, odours and other things, we mistakenly imagine this thirst to be the immediate manifestation of our own essence.

Consciousness is the antecedent condition for the further development and evolution of *nāma-rūpa* or of the corporeal organism. Consciousness must descend into the impregnated ovum in the moment of conception, otherwise it could not develop into an embryo. At this stage consciousness is so weak that it arouses only vegetative irritations, because it is produced by organic matter not yet differentiated to organs of sense. But, as the embryo evolves, consciousness is raised to physical touch-consciousness. Thus the mutual conditionality of both factors, the corporeal organism and consciousness, is established. Each is dependent on the other.

The Buddha defines this consciousness, *viññāṇa*, as an element (*dhātu*) that is "invisible, boundless, all-penetrating". The objects enter this element at the same time, the interlocking of the sensual activities and of their corresponding objects having aroused it.

Only by entering the elements of consciousness are the objects of the senses able to touch us, and only thereby do sensation and perception of them become possible for us. The whole world, therefore, exists for us only as it is irradiated by consciousness, and it vanishes for us as soon as consciousness is extinguished. "Everything has its stand in consciousness" and "When consciousness ceases, this here also ceases."

Through contact of the organ of sense and the immediate object of sense, for instance of the molecular current of the ether striking the surface of the eye, an invisible element called consciousness is aroused. Instantly, with the speed of thought, it spreads along the molecular stream to the object, emanating that stream like an electric current, immediately and completely. Only thus are sensation and perception of the external objects made possible for us, who stand as something inscrutable behind the whole process.

Our unexampled clinging to the body so long as we possess it, and our boundless thirst for a new one the moment we lose it at the moment of death is a thirst which actually leads to a new organism of the same kind, that is, to the formation of a new six-senses-machine.

For the Buddha, conception was more than the sperm of the male uniting with the ovum of the female. He said : "When, monks, a father and mother come together, and it is the mother's period *and the being to be born is also present, then by the combined agency of these three*, a seed of life is planted."[1] Since the Buddha teaches re-birth, it is obvious that "the being to be born" must depart from somewhere. And, of course, the being is from some abandoned body. Thus death and conception are revealed as two sides of the same process. Every conception is only possible through the simultaneous death of another creature in one of the realms of Saṁsāra. What disappears here, re-appears there. To the paroxysms of lust in the moment of coition stand opposed the pangs of death of the creature just conceived.

In this whole matter it must be grasped that, for a dying creature's thirst for existence leading to new grasping of a new germ, the laws of space and of time at that moment do not exist. All the germs in the world are therefore equally near to it. Thirst at this moment is without any substratum, since its former body, upon which it had concentrated itself, has been snatched from it.

At such a moment, free from its former restrictions, it flames up out of the "Nothing", that is, out of our innermost essence, which is as boundless as the universe.

It is obvious that there is a different *direction* of grasping on the death of one being from what there is in another. One creature in dying grasps the ovum of a woman, the other the ovum of an animal womb, another in a hell or in a heaven.

1. *Majj. Nik.*, 38. Discourse

Why, then, this difference ? The answer is : Through the same factor which represents the cause ofgrasping in general, thirst, *taṇhā*. The special kind of thirst, or the main direction taken by will in a dying being, determines not only the grasping itself, but also its direction.

The vital truth here, however, is that *we only grasp what is in harmony with our will.* But we do not always grasp what is in harmony with our willing. This is the case when we recognize the injurious or deceptive nature of that for which we long. Indeed, this recognition, if only it is complete enough, may cure us of our desire for an object and thereby cure us of our grasping at it also. For instance, a man might indulge in alcohol until he sees an alcoholic.

The sight of such a victim might fill the onlooker with such a distaste for alcohol that he never touches it again. Willing is generally modified by *cognition*, inasmuch as in its light we reject objects which in themselves are in harmony with our willing, but are known to us to have injurious consequences. Will affirms itself unchecked only when, in the absence of knowledge, the will is blind. Then, without making any distinction, we grasp at everything that is in harmony with it, regardless of the fact that the object seized will result in the most serious suffering.

At the moment of death, all beings are in this same situation. The will is blind, for *every* kind of consciousness disappears, since their supporters the recently active senses, have ceased to operate. The thirst to maintain oneself in existence, the will to achieve a new Becoming, then affirms itself. Devoid of any kind of cognition, in total blindness, and for this very reason without the least regard to the consequences resulting therefrom, it leads to a grasping at that germ among all possible ones, among the five courses, that is most in harmony with itself. It is because it is in harmony with itself that it grasps at a particular germ, whether the germ is in a human female, in an animal womb, or even in some hell.

Only *later*, when this germ has developed, and with the entry of sense-activity, consciousness again dawns, will the germ seized and adhered to, be illuminated by this same consciousness. Then does the individual recognize himself for what he is.

Because the thirst for new Becoming at the moment of death acts entirely blindly, because of this it acts in accordance with its innermost nature. Thus, at that moment, it is subject to only one law—*the law of affinity*. Thus the striving at death stands in a relationship of affinity only with a certain kind of germ.

Now we not only understand the five groups as representing the complete components of personality, but we also see through their mechanism. The machine is represented by the corporeal organism, the six-sense-machine. It possesses the peculiarity of being able to exist and work only after the accession of another element wholly different from it. This heterogeneous element is consciousness, and it possesses the peculiar quality of being generated anew as soon as the six-sense-machine begins to work.

As soon as it comes alive in this manner, it produces, according to its arousal by the appropriate organ, the sensation of seeing, of hearing, of smelling, of tasting, of touching, of thinking, and the respective perception of the object felt in this way. Out of this sensation and perception the activities of the mind arise.

"In so far only as one can be born, or grow old, or die, or dissolve, or reappear, in so far only is there any process of verbal expression, in so far only is there any process of explanation, in so far only is there any process of manifestation, in so far only is there any sphere of knowledge, in so far only do we go round the wheel of life up to our appearance amid the conditions of this world,—*inasfar as this is, to wit, the corporeal organism together with consciousness*."[1]

The fundamental striving of every animal during its lifetime is restricted to its own kind, all animals having sexual intercourse only with those of their own species. All the more exclusively will this concentration of the will to live upon its own species declare itself at the moment of death, when only a striving to grasp at a similar animal germ will be present, and, accordingly, only grasping at such a germ will take place.

1. *Dīgha Nik.*, XI.

The determination of affinities among mankind will be much more difficult, as, among men, all sorts of directions of the will are represented. There are men with the minds of angels; there are others with minds far below those of the beast. Because of his reason, man may, from a purely objective standpoint, act much worse than any beast. But then his actions, if the other conditions are equal, are, in relation to his reason, always worse than those of an animal. It is clear that a man murdering in spite of his reason, ranks morally far below an animal doing the same without reason.

The Buddha teaches that, from the human realm, paths lead to all the paths of *Saṁsāra.* Thus the thirst for existence of a man with an angel's mind will, when in death he abandons his former organism, draw him to a heavenly world and lead him to a grasping there. Conversely, the base inclinations of a degenerate man, if they alight upon a germ in the animal world akin to themselves, they will grasp this germ. Thus the nature of the future birth of each individual depends upon the direction his desires take during the course of his life until death.

So it is in every case. The striving for a new Becoming to maintain oneself in existence, if it is forced, in consequence of he decay of the body inhabited till now, to search for a new germ, leads to such a grasping as corresponds with the direction already taken during the course of life, in the way that a thrown stone keeps to the direction given to it.

The material substratum of personality is the body, or the six-sense-machine. This machine fitted out with the organs o the senses, and with the means for its further maintenance and continuous supplying with fuel like any other machine, in the womb is built up out of parts of the outer world. These are assimilated by the maternal organism, or changed from dead into vital matter, and so the machine is kept working through an unbroken supply of food. As long as this machine is in order and goes well, it also fulfils its purpose of making possible the element of consciousness and thereby, of sensation and perception and, eventually, the activities of the mind. If it is not able to work anymore, then consciousness too is at an end, along with sensation and perception and, eventually, activities of the mind, because they are mere products of the six-sense-machine and of consciousness.

Only a newly built six-sense-machine could again bring forth these phenomena. Also sensation, perception and the activities of the mind are not persistent, but are only the respective results of the six-sense-machine in conjunction with consciousness and, ultimately, are conditioned by the former. Since, as we have seen, this six-sense-machine, or corporeal organism, is a product of the four chief elements, the five groups constituting personality are thereby causally conditioned: "And thus has the Blessed One spoken: 'Whoso perceives the Arising of things through cause, the same perceives the truth. Who so perceives the truth, the same perceives the Arising of things through cause.' In dependence upon cause, verily, have these five adherence-groups arisen."[1]

Because the body endowed with organs of sense is the apparatus by means of which we come into connection with the world, the body, by coming into action, generating the element of consciousness and only thereby sensation and perception of the world, *the beginning as well as the end of the world is conditioned by it.*

If the body is dissolved by death, the entire world vanishes for us. And if, as the Buddha promises, there is a final overcoming of the world, then we may say that it will be possible only through this, that there exists a way to the final extinguishing of every corporeal organism.

It is on record that Rohitassa, the heavenly spirit, once asked the Blessed One : "May it be possible, O Lord, through going, to know, to see or to reach the end of the world, where neither birth is, nor growing old nor dying, neither originating nor perishing ?"

To this the Buddha replied : "It is impossible, O friend, through going, to know, to see or to reach the end of the world, where neither birth is, nor growing old nor dying, neither originating nor perishing. But neither is it possible to make an end of suffering without having reached the end of the world. But this I declare, O friend: Within this body, six feet high, endowed with perception and cognition, is contained the world, the origin

1. *Majj. Nik.*, 28. Discourse

of the world, and the end of the world, and the path leading towards the end of the world." The Buddha also indicated how this was to be achieved.

"Suppose, monks," he said, "that a monk has won to confidence, virtue, experience, detachment, wisdom, and he heard this saying: 'The thirty-three gods—the shadow gods—the blissful gods—the gods of boundless happiness—the gods dwelling beyond boundless happiness—these live long and gloriously and happily.' Such an one thinks within himself: O that upon the dissolution of the body, after death, I might return to the society of these gods!' This thought he thinks, on this thought he dwells, this thought he cherishes. These creative activities of the mind and the inner conditions that he thus cherishes and promotes within himself, lead to his rebirth in such an existence. This, ye monks, is the way, the transition that leads to return thither."[2]

According to this, man becomes what he wills to become; that is, whatever he desires and thirsts after. For whatever a man thirsts after, that he grasps. Here wishing is not effective here. It is willing and desiring in its innermost depth, in the innermost character, as it appears in action as blind impulse, without being guided by the light of knowledge. For according to the foregoing expositions, our will is in exactly this situation at the decisive moment of death, when it determines our grasping of a new germ.

How can a man be sure that, in the moment of death, when consciousness is lost, that he will, because of his essential nature, make a choice that carries him into a high-placed family or a world of gods? The fundamental condition for the certainty that after death I shall not become attached to a germ in a low-class, pain-laden world, is this: That I know myself, at latest, in the hour of my death, to be finally free of all unworthy inclinations. This must be so absolute that, even in my dreams or even in a state of intoxication, I could not imagine myself so much as drawn towards an act that was anything but selfless, kind and compassionate. In that decisive moment, so pure must the will and character be, that I am drawn only

1. *Ang. Nik.*, IV, 45
2. *Majj. Nik.*, 120. Discourse

to purity and repelled by anything that is base or even remotely ungenerous.

How is the individual to achieve this essential state of will and character? The Buddha answers this crucial question by pointing out that this is the end result of a long period of self-discipline and of self-abnegation. By faithfully pursuing such a course, a man acquires confidence, virtue, experience, detachment, wisdom, and thereby becomes nobler and purer and more adapted to attachment in higher and purer spheres. By incessantly and intensively occupying himself with thoughts that are good and pure and selfless and self-immolating, he turns his entire striving in this direction, until he is wholly absorbed and completely saturated by it. In this state he has developed within him the unshakeable certitude: After death I cannot possibly sink into the depths, but I must rise upwards. Indeed, in that decisive unconscious condition, I can grasp no other germ but the one my being in its very essence desires, as every other would be antithetical to my inmost nature, to the characteristic direction of my will and to my deepest thirst for a definite mode of existence.

As an example of how it is the law of affinity that determines our grasping in death, the thirteenth Discourse of the *Digha-Nikāya* may be cited. In this the way to union with Brahma, the highest aim of the Brahmin caste is, in part, treated like this :

> "The young Brahmin Vāsettha spoke to the Exalted One saying : 'Reverend Gotama, I have heard that the Samana Gotama shows the way that leads to Brahma and to union with him. May the reverend Gotama be pleased to show us this way and lead the Brahmin upwards?'
>
> 'Listen then, Vāsettha, and note well what I shall say.'
>
> 'So be it, Lord,' said the young Brahmin Vāsettha.
>
> The Exalted One spoke and said : 'There the bhikkhu (monk) with his loving mind penetrates one direction of space, and so he penetrates the second and so the third and so the fourth. And thus he penetrates upwards and downwards and horizontally the whole wide world everywhere, completely, with loving benevolent mind, all-embracing, great, beyond all measure, full of peace.

'Just Vāsettha, as a powerful trumpeter easily penetrates all the four regions with the sound of his instrument : even so there remains no restriction for the development of such a benevolent mind thus released. Vāsettha, this is the way leading to Brahma, to union with him.'

'Vāsettha, such a bhikkhu also penetrates with compassionate mind—with joyful mind—with equal mind one direction of space, and so the second and so the third and so the fourth. And thus he penetrates upwards and downwards and horizontally the whole wide world everywhere completely with all-embracing, broad, measureless, compassionate mind, with joyful mind and with equanimity.'

'Just, Vāsettha, as a powerful trumpeter easily penetrates all the four regions with the sound of his instrument; even so there remains no restriction for the development of such a compassionate mind—joyful mind—with equanimity. Vāsettha, this is the way leading to Brahma, to union with him.'

'Now what think you, Vāsettha ? Has the bhikkhu who keeps himself thus, any interest in the petty things of every-day life, or not ?'—'He has not,Reverend Gotama.'—'Is he spiteful or peaceable ?'—'Peaceable, Reverend Gotama.'—'Ill-natured or good-natured ?'—'Good-natured, reverend Gotama.'—'Pure- hearted or impure-hearted ?'—'Pure-hearted, reverend Gotama.'—'Constant or inconstant in his will ?'—'Constant in his will, reverend Gotama.'

"So then, Vāsettha, you say that such a bhikkhu is without interest in the petty things of every-day life, and that Brahma is without interest in the petty things of every-day life. Do these two agree together, a bhikkhu without interest in worldly possessions, and Brahma without interest in worldly possessions ?'—'Yes, reverend Gotama, they agree together.'—'Very good, Vāsettha ! That such a bhikkhu uninterested in worldly things, after the end of his body, after death, should attain to union with Brahma, who is untouched by worldly cares, this is possible.

'And so you say, Vāsettha, that such a bhikkhu is, just like Brahma, peaceable, good-natured, pure-hearted, constant in his will. Do these agree together : a peaceable, good-natured, pure-hearted, constant-willed bhikkhu, and the peaceable, good-natured, pure-hearted, constant-willed Brahma ?'

'Yes, reverend Gotama, they agree together.'

'Very good, Vāsettha ! That therefore such a peaceable, good-natured, pure and constant bhikkhu, after the end of his body, after death, may attain to union with unchanging Brahma— this is possible."

How is this done ? He is by his thirst, his willing, "as it were, conducted" to the heaven of Brahma, as it is said in the 153rd to the 162nd Discourse of the Book of Threes, in the *Aṅguttara-Nikāya.*

It is the law of affinity which dominates and determines the will in its grasping. But in this the law of affinity is not exhausted.

It not only determines generally the germ as a type which will be the subject of the grasping, but it indicates in minutest detail as to why a certain particular germ is seized on and adhered to. Why, for instance, a grasping takes place in the womb of a poor working woman, or of a noble lady, or at a germ already diseased and endowed with but small vitality.

On one occasion a Brahmin asked the Buddha why human beings were so varying in quality, ranging from unspeakable depravity to saintly excellence. To this he gave the reply : "Owners of their works, O Brahmin, are beings, heirs of their works, children of their works, creatures of their works, slaves of their works. Works discriminate beings, according to their depravity and excellence."[1]

Basic to the teaching of the Buddha is the transitory nature of all things, including the four chief elements. In common with all other religions, from the most ancient to the most modern, there is the conviction that the material world will exhaust itself and vanish.

Having stated that the elements are transitory, he then went on to say : "What, then, of this fathom-long body ? Is there aught here of which may rightly be said 'I' or 'Mine' or 'Am'? Nay, verily, nothing whatsoever." The body is

1. Majj. Nik. 135. Discourse

"subject to ruin, destruction, and all vicissitudes." This being so, it is self-evident that the remaining components of our personality are transitory, as they are based upon the body, including its organs of sense :

> "The corporeal form, O monks, is transient and what underlies the arising of the corporeal form, what conditions it, that too is transient. Corporeal form arisen from that which is transient, how could it be permanent?
>
> "Sensation is transient, and what underlies the arising of sensation, what conditions it, that too is transient. Sensation arisen from that which is transient, how could it be permanent?
>
> "Perception is transient, and what underlies the arising of perception, what conditions it, that, too, is transient. Perception arises from that which is transient, how could it be permanent?
>
> "The activities of the mind are transient, and what underlies the arising of the activities of the mind, what conditions them, that, too, is transient. The activities of the mind arisen from that which is transient, how could they be permanent ? ......How could cognition even be permanent?"[1]

It is obvious that it is the law of affinity which determines at which germ there will be the crucial grasping at death.

The man who is so devoid of compassion that he can kill men and animals, carries deep within himself the desire to shorten, life. He finds satisfaction in curtailing the lives of other creatures. He, therefore, has affinity with short-lived germs. And, after his death, he grasps at a germ which is short-lived. Equally, germs bearing within themselves the power of developing into a deformed body, have an affinity for one who finds pleasure in ill-treating and disfiguring others. An angry person begets within himself an affinity for ugly bodies and their respective germs, since it is the characteristic mark of anger to disfigure the face.

The jealous, niggardly and haughty person carries within himself the tendency to grudge everything to others and to despise them. Accordingly, germs destined to develop in poor outward circumstances, possess affinity for him.

1. *Sam. Nik.* XII, 18

What a man has been essentially during his life determines the type of germ at which he will unconsciously grasp after death. The main striving tends in a certain definite direction, and, because of this he develops quite definite and particular qualities of mind. And it is these which are decisive as regards the nature of his grasping at death. But, generally speaking, his thirst, or, as we are more accustomed to say, his willing at the moment of death, is not homogeneous. It is a summation of many and even opposite tendencies. In every man there dwells an angel and a devil. In such a case, what is it which determines the new grasping upon death. The answer is simple. It depends upon whether the good or the bad striving comes into activity at the moment of death and thus determines the new grasping.

And which becomes operative at this crucial moment is decided by the degree of goodness or badness in the will. That, in turn, has been decided by the individual, who has either more given himself up to good deeds, words and thoughts than to bad deeds, words and thoughts.

The individual is subject to the law of gradual becoming. In a world of flux, nothing is stable, not even the character or the will. An individual who is not moving towards greater unselfishness is degenerating into greater selfishness. According to the law of gradual becoming, no one can commit a serious crime, unless his will has long been travelling the road on which it lies. The perpetration of the crime is merely the culmination of a long process of wrong willing. This tendency, of course, remains after the deed is done. It is not the externally visible deed as such, regarded from a purely objective standpoint—for instance the unintentional killing of a man—which determines the future fate of a man. Rather it is the mental disposition in which the deed is performed. That is, it is the direction of will upon which it has followed, whose strengthening is partly conditioned by the very deed.

This is set forth by the Buddha in a dialogue with Upāli, and adherent of Nigantha Nathaputta, in which he says that the man who commits an offence unconsciously is guilty of a greater fault than the one who commits an offence consciously. This is explained by the fact that the man who knows his deed to be detestable, feels the goadings of guilt and is likely to repent. In this way, wickedness does not increase and is likely to diminish. But the man who does evil and is unaware of the fact will be immune from the goadings of guilt and is unlikely to repent. Thus, in him, evil is likely to increase. In another saying the Buddha declares a man who unconsciously does evil to be free of fault—"*ajānantassa n'āpatti*: without knowledge no fault"—thus refers to an objective error in opposition to ignorance of the moral law or *karma.* This is illustrated by the following from the Sūtrakṛtāṅga :

> "If a savage throws his spear through the side of corn-stack, believing it to be a man, or through a pumpkin, believing it to be a child, and roasts it, then he is guilty of murder, according to our view. But if a savage spears a man and roasts him, believing it to be a pumpkin, then he is not guilty of murder, according to our view."

According to this, every act of volition leads to certain quite definite consequences, not only consisting in those which manifest themselves in the present life, and called by the Buddha the "visible chain of suffering", but manifesting themselves also beyond death as the "hidden chain of suffering". For every act of volition determines by way of the tendency of will, conditioned or partly conditioned or strengthened by it, the grasping of one of our future rebirths and thus contributes towards our transference into the corresponding external circumstances. This effectuation of all willing, in accordance with law, called the law of Karma in the Dialogues, is also called "the fruit of deeds", or simply the law (*dharma*).

It was in the transitory nature of all things that the Buddha found life's ineradicable anguish. He said, "....whatever is transient, that is painful." And so, with the body, sensation, perception, activities of the mind and cognition, because they are transient, they are painful. This painfulness, caused by transitoriness, shows itself in the body as "decay" and "death", and in the four other groups as "pain, sorrow, grief and despair."

Thus, at last, there remains of every satisfaction of will, nothing but suffering caused by its loss. Only with this final effect can it be entered up in the book of life. The latter, therefore, at last, must show nothing but negative entries. In fact, the Buddha is right in valuing everything ultimately as suffering. Yesterday with all its pleasures, is no more than a mere shadow. And to-morrow, to-day will be just such another shadow. And so must it be with all our days until, at last, face to face with death, our entire life is seen to be no more than a shadow.

This will-to-live has one final resource to save itself modifying its judgment on the value of life. The individual may comfort himself with the thought that the fruits of his labours. pains and troubles, will be reaped by his relatives, and also by mankind as a whole. In this way he may feel he has made a contribution to the general good. Certainly mankind rises ever higher, until the superior civilization falls a victim to the law of dissolution and decay, as has happened countless times during the limitless past.

Thereupon the play begins anew, and continues through endless time, only interrupted by world-catastrophes, in which, everything, including the whole staging of life disappears because the planets fall into the sun, until the staging is built anew. But meanwhile every individual perishes through inevitable death again and again. *For there is no evolution such as Western man imagines.* In life, death is as essential as birth, old age as essential as youth. And there is no evolution of the world that is not inevitably followed by decay. Evolution and decay are simply two aspects of the same process—the process of *becoming*. Everything appears in the first part of its *becoming* as evolution, in the second part as decay.

The impossibility of achieving any lasting satisfaction of will, which prevails throughout the whole world, means that suffering dominates. This is so obvious that it can in no wise be refuted. But it can be ignored. Indeed, incredible though it is, the will of man is so strong that it enables him to ignore even this fundamental truth if he is determined not to see it. By means of empty sophisms he blunts the impact of the wounding truth and even babbles in high-sounding phrases about reaching a final state in which mankind is full of bliss.

Rightly understood, the law of Karma is nothing more than the law of causality, both in its formal meaning as the law of cause and effect, and in its material significance, according to which a certain quite definite effect inevitably follows upon a certain definite cause. But it is not-limited to the physical world. It reigns with equal exactness in the moral world, and therefore beyond death. In this, its all-embracing sphere of validity, it is that power, now marvelled at as benevolent providence, now feared as the dark fate, to which is subject every act of will, even the slightest in the faintest thought. The moment any kind of volition stirs, it stirs in harmony with the law of causality, or else not at all.

Because of this law of Karma we cannot escape our deeds. They will inevitably find us at the proper time in the form of their effects. "Nowhere in the world is there a place where a man can escape his own evil deeds."[1]

"Commit a crime, and the world is made of glass."[2] Our present body, together with all its sense organs and mental faculties, is exclusively a product of our previous actions, inasmuch as this has brought about the grasping in the maternal womb. "This is not, ye disciples, your body nor the body of another, rather must it be regarded as the deed of the past, the deed that has come to fruition, the deed that is willing actualized, that has become perceptible."[3] And again : "My deeds are my possession, my deeds are my inheritance, my deeds make the womb that bears me, my deeds determine the family to which I am related, my deeds are my refuge."[4]

The consequences of our willing are regulated by an inescapable law. Law reigns absolute in the realm of morality even as it reigns absolute in the realm of nature. Nay, the two are one. The moral and the natural laws are but different aspects of the same law which runs right through the universe, visible and invisible. Just as conception leads to birth, as deprivation of air leads to asphyxiation, so every action of will and, accordingly, every kind of grasping leads to its corresponding consequences in the corresponding kind of Becoming. The Buddha drew attention to this fact when he said :

"Whoever, Bhumija, being an ascetic or a Brahmin, cog-

1. The *Dhammapada*, V. 127
2. Emerson, Essays
3. *Sam. Nik.*, XII, 37
4. *Aṅg. Nik.*, V, 57

nizes wrongly, or acts wrongly....and thus perhaps with hope leads the life of an ascetic, cannot possibly reach the goal, and thus perhaps without hope leads an ascetic life, cannot possibly reach the goal......And why not? Because they do not from the very foundation understand how to reach the goal."[1]

The Buddha taught that life is without beginning or end, unless we make an end to it : "Without beginning or end, ye monks, is this round of rebirth (*saṁsāra*). There cannot be discerned a first beginning of beings who, sunk in ignorance and bound by thirst, ceaselessly transmigrating, again and again run to a new birth." *Saṁsāra* means : *sar*, a course, *sam*, returning to its starting point. It is only from this standpoint that the flood of suffering, the dreadfulness and awfulness of life is to be seen in its full measure.

The round of rebirths, within which the enmeshed creature wanders incessantly, consists of five fates. These are : "Passage into the hell-world, the animal kingdom, the realm of shades, the world of men or the abodes of the gods."

Which of the five worlds a man enters after the break-up of his body, after death, is determined by the nature of his thirsting, of his willing, during his life. By his conduct does a man determine his fate in his next existence.

The one who has the misfortune to so live that he has, after death, only affinity with that germ which consigns him to the hell-world, is in a truly sorry state. The Buddha described it in terms which must make the stoutest heart quail. He said : "....what a man, chastised daily with three hundred strokes of a sword, experiences of sadness and sorrow, cannot be reckoned, counted or compared against the sufferings of the hell-worlds."

Nor is the man who, in a new birth, descends to the status of an animal in much better case. For he has little chance indeed of returning to the world of men. "And why so?" the Buddha asked. And he answered : "Because (in the animal world) there is no just conduct, no straightforward conduct, no wholesome acting, no charitable acting. There, monks, they are accustomed to devour each other, and to kill the weaker ones."

1. *Majj. Nik.*, 126. Discourse

As for the man in the realm of shades, the Buddha describes him as sore afflicted and distressed, but he does not specify the nature of the torments.

The one who is reborn as a human being he describes, naturally, as sharing the common human lot, while the man who achieves the heaven-worlds "enjoys the height of felicity."[1]

Among these five fates ultimately only the last one—the abode in the heaven-world—could be desirable. But, according to the Buddha, this one is just as much subject to the law of transitoriness as are the other four abodes. He said ; "Up to the highest world of the gods every existence becomes annihilated—the Thirty-three Gods and the Yāma Gods, the satisfied Gods, the Gods who Delight in Fashioning, the Gods Who Have Control of Pleasures Fashioned by Others, they all, bound with the fetters of desire, return into the power of Māra which means into the power of death." Unfailingly, therefore, descent to the lower worlds again must follow.[2]

But this pleasant prospect of staying in a heaven, or even only in the realm of mankind, is open to only very few beings.

"These three, ye disciples, will fall a prey to the abyes and to hell. He who lives unchastely and pretends to be chaste; he who accuses a chaste-living disciple of unchaste living; he who, believing and thinking that there is nothing evil in sensuality, falls a prey to sensual pleasure. These three, ye disciples, will fall a prey to the abyss and to hell, *if they do not abstain from these things.*"[3]

A certain person who has committed only a small crime may find that this brings him to hell. The Buddha said: "But of which kind is the man whom a small crime which he has committed brings to hell? A man who has not won insight into the ego, has not practised himself in virtue, has not developed his mind, not awakened knowledge, is narrow-minded, small-minded, and so has to suffer in consequence of trifles. Such a man, ye disciples, even a small crime which he has committed may bring to hell.

1. *Majj. Nik.*, 12. Discourse
2. Cp. *Sam. Nik.*. V, 7
3. *Aṅg. Nik.*, III, 111

"But of which kind is the man in whom the same small crime which he has committed will ripen even during his life-time, and in whom not even a small effect (after death) ensues, to say nothing of a great one? There, ye disciples, a man has won insight into the ego, has practised himself in virtue, has developed his mind, has awakened knowledge, is broad-minded, magnanimous, dwelling in the Immeasurable. In such a man, ye disciples, the same small crime which he has committed ripens even during his life-time, and not even a small effect manifests itself (after death) to say nothing of a great one."

Whether the consequences of a deed shall extend up to the death-moment and thereby into the next existence, is determined exclusively by the extent to which the deed affects the will. A vain, narrow-minded man will feel what is the mildest criticism as a serious assault upon his self-conceit, which he will be unable ever to pardon sincerely and from the heart. Thus it will leave inextinguishable traces within him. On the other hand, upon a noble-hearted man, who is convinced of the worthlessness of all worldly things, a most serious insult will make not the least impression. Should a most unjust or ungrateful attitude excite him, it will do so only briefly.

And the influence upon his will, brought about by this excitement, will very soon ripen into repentance, work itself out, and through the kindness and compassion dwelling within him, will have ceased to have any effect upon him whatsoever. The effect will be taken out of him, root and branch, so that at his death nothing will remain which might influence the next grasping. Kindness and compassion are the "Immeasurables" mentioned above, wherein all egotism is dissolved, as is a lump of salt in the river Ganges.

Thereby also the way is shown, not how we may escape from the consequences of our evil actions of the past, for, as is obvious from what has already been said, this is impossible. But we can confine these consequences to our *present* life, or, at least, weaken their post-mortem consequences. We only need to annihilate or, at least, to weaken the evil dispositions of our will, the bad qualities of our character which have grown out of our evil deeds, and which, at bottom, represent nothing but the sum of these, in which therefore, in some mysterious manner, we carry about with us the continuously active force of each former evil deed.

Precisely because of this in our heavy labours of soul for the complete annihilation or weakening of several, or of all our bad qualities, we also kill our former evil deeds themselves. "Outlive them one after the other," as it is said in the "Book of Threes." So that in the same proportion that we are freed from a certain bad quality of character, we also are freed from the further consequences of the deeds related to this quality.

The Buddha taught that the number of rebirths were beyond calculation, and he warned, ".....only a few creatures who have died as men are reborn as men....far more come back to existence in a hell, among animals, or in the realm of the shades."[1]

Thus every being is eternally wandering to and fro within *Saṁsāra*, through the five realms, finding itself reborn by the incessant change of the five groups constituting its personality, now as a man, now as a spectre, now as an animal, now as a devil, now and then as a god. There is, in fact, unless the essential action is taken to escape, an endless wandering through the worlds. "Without beginning or end is this round of rebirths."

"And thus, O monks," the Buddha said, "during a long time you have experienced suffering, you have experienced pain and misery and have enlarged the burying-ground, truly long enough to be disgusted with all productions, long enough to turn away from them."[2]

The anguish suffered is beyond description:

"What do you think, O monks? Which may be more, the flood of tears you have shed on this long way, running again and again to new birth and new death, united to the disliked, separated from the liked, complaining and weeping, or the water of the four great oceans?....

"Through a long time, you have experienced the death of the mother, the death of the father, the death of the son, the death of the daughter, the death of brother and sister, the loss of wealth, the pain of sickness was your lot, while you

1. *Aṅg. Nik.*, I, 19
2. *Sam. Nik.*, XV, 1

were united to the disliked, separated from the liked, running from birth to death, from death to birth, you have shed on this long way truly more tears than water is contained within the four great oceans."[1]

All this suffering is due to the rebirths imposed on the individual by his evil inclinations, and the Buddha points out how these evil inclinations can be completely annihilated. From which it follows that, whoso follows this way faithfully and to the end, need have no further anxiety on account of the later fruits of his former evil life, or of his former evil lives. The one who faithfully follows this path, at the last becomes so full of inner happiness, he may cry out: "Escaped am I from hell, escaped am I from the animal kingdom, escaped from the realm of the shades, escaped from the evil track, escaped from the path of suffering, from the rejected world! I have entered the stream (that leads to the 'Deathless'). Sure am I never again to sink back to the abodes of misery. With unalterable resolve I turn my mind to making myself ripe for the knowledge that delivers."[2]

This consoling confidence may only be reached by him who, in the right manner as laid down by the Buddha, wages warfare for the gradual eradication, or at least the weakening, of his passions. It is not enough merely to be good in the sense of keeping in check bad qualities of character and cultivating the good ones. For the former still remain as bearers of our earlier bad deeds.

There merely take place no *new* evil deeds, undesirable fruits, but only good actions which in time will bear their good fruits. But because the evil actions of a former existence, manifesting themselves in present bad qualities of character, still remain in existence, it may well happen that a man who only in this sense has been good during his immediate past has kept his bad qualities in check without annihilating them or without appreciably weakening them. After death, because of his former evil deeds, such a man may pass to a hell-world. Conversely, a bad man, in consequence of his good actions in

1. *Sam. Nik.*, XV, 1
2. *Sam. Nik.*, XII, 5

a previous lifetime, may at death, capitalize, as it were on the good qualities of his character and rise to a heaven-world.

It is also shown how, on other grounds, a good man may come into a hell, and a bad one into a heaven. The former may occur, for example, if a man otherwise good during his life, loses patience during his last wearisome illness and becomes fretful and quarrelsome. A bad one may go to heaven when, for example, a criminal comes to his senses on the scaffold. In both cases, strivings are called into life which are dominative in the moment of death, and which, therefore, determine the new grasping. But the good or evil strivings latent at this dying moment and thereby ineffectual, through cultivated during the rest of the life, will determine a *later* future.

According to this, the harvest of our doings is certain, but, in its details, the course of Karma is for most men wholly uncertain because of its extreme complexity. This complexity is such that "the fruit of deeds" is one of the "four inscrutable things about which one ought not to brood, because who broods about them will fall a prey to delusion or mental disturbance."[1]

The only thing now needed is to know how our actions must be shaped in accordance with the law of Karma, if they are to bear us good fruit and lead to a fortunate rebirth. Or what for us is wholesome (*kuśala*), and what unwholesome (*akuśala*)? Thus we come to the problem of good and evil. For good is what is wholesome for us; bad or evil is what is unwholesome for us.

The law of Karma acts in the form of affinity, every rebirth taking place through a grasping at the moment of death. The grasping is determined by the tendencies of will prevailing at the moment of death, which in their totality give *taṇhā*, thirst. According to this, the actions which create those tendencies of will that lead to grasping in a joyless world are unwholesome, while those that lead to grasping in a joyful world are wholesome or good.

The Buddha's doctrine embraces three statements:

1. There is an existence after death;

1. *Aṅg. Nik.*, IV, 77

2. This existence is effected by rebirth, strictly speaking, by palingenesis;
3. It takes place within the five realms already mentioned.

The first statement has always been accepted as true by the immense majority of mankind. Men echo the claim of Spinoza: "We feel by immediate consciousness that we are immortal." Only when men try to transfer this immediate truth, founded in the depth of their essence, into abstract knowledge—that is, when they try to understand it in accordance with the law of sufficient reason—do contradictions appear.

According to the Buddha, there are, "....bad actions which bear bad fruits, good actions which bear good fruits, and action partly good and partly bad which bear fruits partly good and partly bad."

The man who practises pain-full (bad) actions in deeds, words and thoughts, comes back to existence in a pain-full world. In such a world, he is touched by pain-full things.

Thus the bad actions bear bad fruits. On the other hand, good actions bear good fruits. These are pain-free actions in deeds, words and thoughts, and the man who practises them comes back to existence in a pain-free world. He is, of course, touched by pain-free things. So, too, with the man who practises actions which are partly pain-full and partly pain-free in deeds, words and thoughts. He returns to existence in a world partly pain-full and partly pain-free, and is touched by things partly pain-full and partly pain-free.[1]

The outstanding thing about the pain-laden worlds, hell and the animal Kingdom, is that the creatures in them recognise in themselves no limit to the thirst for existence and well-being which animates them, and in its coarsest form. On the contrary, they so completely identify themselves with this thirst in its two main manifestations—namely, desire for everything corresponding to it, and hatred for everything opposed to it—that in order to satisfy it they encroach on the sphere of other creâture's interests.

But the inhabitants of the joyful worlds, the heavens,

1. *Aṅg. Nik.*, 231 and 232

are free from such desire and such hate. Above all, they do not satisfy their desires at the expense of other creatures. On the contrary, they include these beings with an ever more comprehensive love in their own thirst for well-being, which thus in them takes a new direction. The reason for this is that in these realms the delusion that our essence is identical with our personality, and that our thirst for well-being ought therefore to be concentrated on it, is partly overcome. Thus the wall of partition dividing ourselves from other creatures is partly thrown down. Thus desire, hatred and delusion appear as the characteristics of the lower and woeful worlds, while desirelessness, freedom from hatred and right insight characterise the higher worlds, whose inhabitants tread a path of ever-expanding love. Between both stands what is specifically human. Desire (*lobha*), hate (*doṣa*) and delusion (*moha*) are unwholesome or bad for us. Conversely, desirelessness (*alobha*), freedom from hatred (*adoṣa*) and non-delusion (*amoha*) are wholesome or good for us. In these fundamental qualities are contained all virtues and all vices.

Existence is conditioned through *the thirst* for existence which animates us, and the shaping of the outer conditions of this existence may be traced back to *the character* of this thirst. We are in this world because we thirsted for it. We are here precisely because we had a thirst which, according to the eternal laws, led us inevitably into this world. Thus we need only annihilate this thirst within ourselves, and thereby prevent any future rebirth, and so, at our next death, depart out of this world forever.

But is it possible to annihilate this thirst for existence? Is it not a manifestation of the very essence of the individual, and for that reason not to be annihilated except when the essence is annihilated? The Buddha insisted that this thirst is not of the essence of the individual, since in it can be observed a rising and a passing away. But this criterion for the recognition of the sphere of *anātta*, of not-self, cannot be accepted at once. For the thirst for existence and wellbeing fills us from our first moment and continues, unceasingly and powerfully, through all our repeated existences. A hypothesis cannot be correct if it is contrary to a fundamental fact of the course of nature.

But to this course of nature there belongs not only man and all his activities, but also the immediate consciousness of living on after death. Thus it must be included in an explanation of life. Many claim that the longing to live on after death is peculiar to man and is bound to be frustrated. But the fact that such a longing is present in every man and so is essential to us, gives surety for the realization of this longing in some way or other, in accordance with the axiom, Nature makes nothing in vain. We could not possess this longing if it were not to be satisfied.

In any case, materialism is already wrecked on the fact of the existence of moral—that is, unselfish—actions. They belong as much to the phenomena of life as birth and death. Even the materialist esteems a man who sacrifices his person for others. But how can he reconcile this esteem with his own doctrine, according to which it must be senseless to annihilate oneself, to save the life of someone who is nothing to me. For what bond, according to materialism, can bind me to this man? Am I not a fool to sacrifice my life for another person, since, in accordance with the materialistic view of the world, life must be my most precious possession, and I lose everything when my life is lost.

The materialist has a universe without values—which are the very things which dominate human thought, attitude and action. Indeed, men sacrifice material possessions because they feel impelled to do so by moral obligation. Du Prel said:

> "Man is the highest fact of nature, and morality is his highest function. Instinctively we place morality higher than knowledge.... Consequently, the real test of philosophical systems is their aptitude for forming the basis of a moral system. But moral instinct is illogical if human individuality exists only between the cradle and the grave. If the visible part of our career alone had validity, and we went towards our annihilation with full consciousness, then we should resemble men condemned to death...."

The Buddha also challenges the materialistic doctrine that, with death all is over. He said, "If it (the materialistic doctrine) is true, then every moral action is purposeless."

Indeed, the knowledge that materialism makes all *true*

morality impossible, is decisive in causing every moral man to refuse it. The moral man immediately feels the overriding importance of moral action and rejects materialism merely from this immediate feeling. For felt truth is nothing but truth immediately perceived, but not yet abstracted into notions. And it is only to men who have gained this level of moral action does the Buddha address himself.

If the fact of death not being our end is established, then there arises the further question: Of what kind is his continued existence after death? The Christian believes the individual continues to exist in an eternal heaven or an eternal hell. The Buddha, however, taught the doctrine of palingenesis. From this it is clear of what decisive importance is the proof that 'thirst' is *nothing metaphysical*, but is subject in every respect to causality! It is conditioned and is, therefore, something *purely physical*; that is, *anattā*, not-the-Self. For if thirst were the essence of man, and thereby the Self, then through all eternity there could be no deliverance from it, nor from suffering, since no one can annihilate himself.

Were this the case, the doctrine of the Buddha would become meaningless, since its very heart consists in pointing out a way of deliverance that may be trodden at all times and speedily leads to the goal, if the necessary attention is applied to its treading. It is ridding oneself of this thirst which is so basic to all the teaching of the Buddha.

He asked, "On what is (this) thirst dependent?" and he replied, "In dependence on *sensation* arises thirst." Without the stimulus of *sensation* there is no desire. When every sensation has vanished completely and forever, then all willing and all thirst of every kind is also gone forever. This thirst is dependent on the sensation of eye-contact, ear-contact, nose-contact, tongue-contact, body-contact and mind-contact. Thus contact gives rise to sensation. In turn, contact is dependent on the *corporeal organism* (*nāma-rūpa*).

It is obvious that the body perishes in death, its components returning to the common stock of inorganic substances of external nature. With the body perish the components of personality—namely, sensation, perception, mentation and cognition. This being true, and the fact of life after death being true, all doctrines of personal continuation after death must be rejected.

The only possibility of continuation *involves the annihilation of personality*. This annihilation is contained in palingenesis, which means decomposition and renewal of the entire personality. Thus the dying creature perishes entirely, together with its consciousness, but there remains a germ from which a new personality arises together with new consciousness. Thus the pain of dependence ultimately comes to its end in the "corporeal organism together with consciousness", wherewith, indeed, in the Mahā-Nidāna-Sutta it reaches its definite conclusion. The reason for this is that the circle of dependence is actually closed.

We can only escape for ever from suffering when we succeed in leaving behind forever Saṁsāra, the circle of rebirth. Then we are no longer exposed to a further new birth, and so to no new formation of the "corporeal organism together with consciousness." For the moment the process by which this new formation is accomplished, for the entire duration of the existence of this newly forming "body endowed with consciousness," we are again indissolubly bound to it. Only at the moment of ensuing death can we entirely step out of Saṁsāra.

Thus all suffering is founded in the "corporeal organism together with consciousness",or the six-senses-machine in general the machine of suffering in particular. These two united—"the body endowed with consciousness"—are the consequence of our thirst for existence during the existence previous to our most recent birth, which existence had as its antecedent condition "a corporeal organism together with consciousness", and so on backwards to all eternity.

The content of the formula of causality may be summed up succinctly as follows: Personality in both its main groups, the corporeal organism, together with consciousness as its real substratum, is conditioned by thirst, and thirst by our bygone personality. So astonishingly simple is the formula of origination by dependence.

The root of suffering is fully laid bare. We have penetrated to the unwearied builder of our corporeal organism itself, through which, as through the machine of suffering, all suffering becomes primarily possible for us. At the same time, we have recognized this builder of the machine of suffering as a fellow who has nothing at all to do with our true essence, to whom therefore we need only hand his passports in order to be free for ever from any new reincarnation.

We are now ready to understand the second of the four holy truths: "This is the most excellent truth of the origination of suffering: it is thirst generating rebirth, thirst accompanied by pleasure and lust, now here and there taking delight, thirst for sensual pleasure, thirst for Becoming (for existence), thirst for annihilation."[1]

The thirst for annihilation arises in consequence of the wrong view that the ego is our essence. For if we recognize that this personality as such is full of suffering, then the further notion arises that we can free ourselves from suffering only by the annihilation of our personality and thereby of our essence. Accordingly, the *thirst* for annihilation arises.

This theory of continuance after death stands in no contradiction to any other fact of the course of nature. This fact can hardly be controverted, as it is in harmony with the whole process of nature. So true is this that even Hume, though "excessively empirical," says in his sceptical treatise on immortality that this system is the only one of its kind to which philosophy can pay heed.

Reincarnation, in fact, has always been the conviction of the choicest and wisest of mankind. But *how* this renewal of existence effects itself in the moment of death is the great mystery. And nobody has effected its solution as completely and convincingly as the Buddha. Such was the genius of his insight that he was able to look into nature's most secret workshop. As soon as we have reached the insight that reincarnation is the real form of our living on, then we are aware that our rebirths had no beginning. As the birth that opened our present life was not the first, then neither was the one which preceded it, nor was the one before that, and so on without cessation, back to the beginningless infinity of the past.

Just as the Buddha divined the eternal nature of time, so he divined the further truth, and one that is quite in harmony

1. *Sam. Nik.*, LVI, 11

with modern astronomy, that the universe consists of countless world-systems and therefore of countless earths. Thus the human being is the heir to all time and to the whole universe.

The formula of causality is extended still further. After the causal nexus has been traced back to the corporeal organism —*nāma-rūpa* and this latter has been declared to be conditioned by consciousness, this consciousness is not again represented as conditioned by the corporeal organism. Instead, it is said: "In dependence upon the *Saṅkhārā* arises consciousness. In dependence upon ignorance arises the *Saṅkhārā.*" It is clear this conclusion of the formula is not to surpass "the corporeal organism together with consciousness," if it is not to contradict what we have hitherto been learning. For, since the conclusion as we have been learning to know it, turns back again to the beginning, a further continuance of the dependences beyond it, is thus quite impossible.

Sankhārā is derived from the verb *saṅkharoti,* an equivalent of the Latin verb *conficere,* meaning literally "to make (together)", i.e. "to put together". Hence its *participium praeteritum* means "put together", "joined together", in the sense of "made", "created", "produced". According to the Canon, it can be used of everything, for everything is *saṅkhata,* that is, joined together, created and produced.

The material out of which it is put together are the six elements, earth, water, fire, air, space, consciousness, which, according to the Buddha, are the only components of the world.

The substantive verb pertaining to *saṅkhata* is Saṅkhārā, which means "the making together", "the putting together", "the producing". "The saṅkhārā derive their name from the fact that they produce (*saṅkharonti*) what is *saṅkhata.*" Thus the concept saṅkhārā is as all-comprising as that of saṅkhata. Everything is *saṅkhata,* "brought forth", "produced", and everything which is *saṅkhata* is based upon a *saṅkhārā,* an "act of producing". Although *saṅkhārā* means, first of all, the act of bringing forth, produced, it may as well be used in the sense of *saṅkhata,* just as the word "production" denotes both the action of producing and that which has been produced.

The Buddha was most deeply exercised in mind by the knowledge that all productions are transitory. It is a theme basic to his whole thinking.

"Transient are the productions (*saṅkhārā*), unsteady are the productions, troublesome are the productions; it suffices to get weary of all productions, it suffices to shrink back from them, it suffices to detach oneself from them....It is sufficient to get disgusted at all productions, sufficient to abhor them, sufficient to become detached from them." The latter strong terms are repeated at least four times within a very short space.

According to the Buddha, everything in the world is a mere "Production", originating and vanishing. He deols with these productions in particular only insofar as there is something arising from *us*, whose unfathomable essence lies beycnd this world, and as this world with its "painful things" comes into contact with *us*. "Here in the consciousness stands the universe." As soon as each kind of consciousness disappears for lack of sensual activity, all the world has vanished for us, too. As the Buddha says: "Just in this body, six feet high, endowed with perception and consçiousness, the world is contained, the origin of the world, the end of the world, and the path leading to the end of the world."

To this body we come through seizing an impregnated ovum in a mother's womb, driven by our Thirsting Will. This embryo develop, forming our body in the way of *Becoming*. But there is no explanation as to which principle compels the material substances to take the form of the corporeal organism, with its organs of sense in such a way that they are able to produce consciousness and therewith the phenomenon of life. This teleology of Becoming also remains an insoluble enigma for modern science. This restricts itself to the statement that all Becoming is executed by those natural processes of a purely physico-chemical nature. This explains nothing. For the Latin word *processus* simply means "occurrence". Thus, science cannot explain or even identify the "something" which is the agency "by which the material is brought into the form, here of rock-crystal, there into that of a lion, there into that of a man."

The Buddha solves this problem. Having asserted that the Becoming of the corporeal organism is conditioned by the accession of consciousness, he asserts: "In dependence on the *Productions* (*saṅkhārā*) arises consciousness." This means that the Productions form the germ seized in a mother's womb into the corporeal organism.

They form it into that apparatus which, by its six organs of sense, makes possible sensations, perceptions, creative mental activities and cognition. "The *sankhārā* (the productions) are called so because they produce (*abhisaṅkharenti*) that which is *saṅkhata* (*produced*). They produce the corporeal shape for corporeality's sake as a product, sensation for sensation's sake as a product, perception for perception's sake as a product, mental creative activities for creative mental activities' sake as a product."

Thus the Buddha dissolved the Becoming of the entire machinery of personality into a heap of Productions. The nun Vajīrā said: "Why do you cling to the word 'being'? *There is nothing else but a heap of productions.*

If, after the manner of Descartes, I ask proof that I am, then the Buddha provides such proof, and, in accordance with the self-evident nature of the fact to be proved, it is the most striking that could be given: "You are, because you suffer." He was then compelled to ask:

Is the necessity of suffering grounded in our essence, suffering being merely an emanation of the same? Or is it something that reaches us only as an alien element?" Only if it is the latter is there possibility of freeing ourselves from it. If it is in our essence, we can no more escape than our hand can throw itself away.

It was precisely through this problem of suffering and the problem of its annihilation that the Buddha found himself confronted by the great question: What is the proper essence of man? Or, what is his true Self? The importance of this question is so great that he has placed the answer to it in the very heart of his doctrine.

He explained that, behind the productions stands the will of the individual, and the productions serve the will. He said: "The Five Groups of Grasping are rooted in the Will."[2] And: "In the *Will* all things are rioted."[3] With considerable em-

1. *Sam. Nik.*, XXII, 79
2. *Majj. Nik.*, 109 Discourse
3. *Aṅg. Nik.*, X, 58

phasis the will is pointed out as the fountain of productions: "The ordinary man, not knowing the doctrine, regards the Five Groups of Grasping as himself. This opinion is a production.. When the ordinary man is hit by a sensation started from a contact taking place in the state of ignorance, *Thirst* arises within him. From this results the production."[1] This explanation holds good for *all* the productions constituting personality. Thus the real constructor of the body, and of the total personality is this *Thirst* or desire.

"No longer will my mind create anew,
Since ghastly thirsting is destroyed, for true."[2]

In the 28th Discourse of the *Majjh. Nik.* the body is described as a "construction of thirst". The productions are simply the *executors of the will.* The productions set to work to satisfy this Will, and where the Will wants nothing more, then there are no more productions.

The productions are *our* productions, as the Thirsting Will is our will. Accordingly, each man is the *demiurge* himself forming the stuff into the corporeal organism with its six organs of sense and creating for itself, by and within this consciousness, his world. But the world alas, is nothing but a suffering creation.

In spite of the artistic skill displayed in the productions, there is a fundamental insufficiency of the working-stuff; i.e. in the material of which our corporeal organism and all the world presenting itself within consciousness, consists. This is the transitoriness of this stuff. And so these words will remain true forever:

"Whatever is produced, will pass away; once it will perish, as it was brought forth. If every Production is left off, man's welfare is attained for good."[3]

"And now, ye monks, take it for granted: Whatever one may produce—it must vanish again. So you have to struggle indefatigably for the aim (of producing nor more)."[4]

"These three marks of the Produced are there: Arising is

1. *Sam. Nik.*, XII, 81
2. *Dhamm.*, V, 157
3. *Digha. Nik.*, XVI, 6 and 10
4. *Ibid.*, 7

showing itself; perishing is showing itself; and during its existence mutation is showing itself."[1]

So far we have come to know two classes of "Productions". The first comprises everything arisen at all; the second embraces the entire machinery of personality. That is, the totality of those Five Groups of Grasping into which the Buddha has dissolved personality. "The Five Groups of Grasping are the personality."[2] Yet there remains a third class of *saṅkhārā*. This is the sum of the fourth Group of Grasping, also called *saṅkhārā*. Which peculiar productions are summarized in the fourth Group of Grasping? In order to answer this question the first three Groups of Grasping must be eliminated. Then the remaining part of the personality's machinery renders the only possible contents of the last two Groups of Grasping—i.e. the "productions". (*saṅkhārā*) and "cognition" (*viññāṇa*). In addition to the first Three Groups of Grasping—corporeal form, sensation, perception—only thinking remains. "What one senses, one perceives; what one perceives, one thinks." Thus the last two Groups of Grasping must consist in thinking. And this fourth Group of Grasping is the *producing* thinking. It is the thinking employed by the Thirsting Will, incessantly striving to satisfy this Thirsting Will that it might not torment us permanently.

In every change something perishes, and something new is formed. But what has perished cannot be unhappy as it no longer exists. Nor can the something newly arisen be unhappy, as it has not experienced the change, but has only just arisen out of it. In any case, it ought to feel glad about this change, as it owes its existence to it. Therefore a third something must be present which feels the change to be painful. This third something *I* am. Accordingly the Buddha makes the following formula the criteria for determining the boundary between Self and Not-Self: What I perceive originating and perishing, that cannot be my I, my Self, as what I perceive to originate and to perish must, logically, be something different from me. Just because I exist, I cannot be that which I perceive disappear before myself a *the perceiving subject*. For were the Self identical

1. *Aṅg. Nik.*, III, 47
2. *Majj. Nik.*, 44. Discourse

with the disappearing object, when it disappeared, I should have disappeared also. But I am still here after the thing has gone. Therefore it was not my I nor anything belonging to me which disappeared. On the contrary, it is its disappearance that causes me astonishment, surprise and pain.

It is through my not-myself being involved in this passing away that pain and suffering, in consequence of transitoriness, become possible. This presupposes something to exist which *experiences* this passing from the state desired into the state not desired, which, therefore, does not itself participate in this incessant change. This something is nothing but myself. I cannot be identical with the cause of my pains. Were I identical with the thing I behold perish, I could not experience pain through this passing away. For whatever in its own essence is transitory—and everything I see to be transitory is so because of its own inner nature—cannot experience this transitoriness as painful, *since it is not contrary to its nature to be transitory, but only the outcome of its innermost essence.* Thus the Buddha's second criterion for determining the boundary between Self and Not-Self is self-evident. It is that *I cannot consist in that which, because of its transitoriness, causes me pain.*

This compares perfectly with the form in which Schopenhauer has rendered the paralogism of personality given by Kant.

"With regard to all motion, of whatever kind it may be it can be stablished *a priori* that it becomes perceivable only by comparison with something at rest. From this it follows that the course of time also, together with everything within it, could not be perceived if there were not something that had no part in the same, with the motionless of which we contrast the motion of time....Next we cannot imagine, if everything within our consciousness was going on together at once in the ordinary flow of time, how this going on could nevertheless be perceived. For this to happen we must assume something to remain at rest, at which time with its contents flows past. Therefore there must be something immovable within consciousness itself. This can be nothing but the perceiving subject itself gazing unmoved and unchanging at the course of time and its changing play.... The truth is, that even in our empirical consciousness *an eternal resting-point may be pointed out, but only one point, and that it may only just be pointed out....*

Here I refer to my own doctrine, according to which the recognizing subject is all-perceiving but cannot be perceived."[1]

The criteria for determining the realm of Not-Self—to wit perceived transitoriness and the suffering which arises from this transitoriness, in the Discourses are always condensed into this logical sequence: That which is transient is painful. That which is transient, painful and subject to all vicissitudes cannot be regarded as my Self.

Accordingly, what is Not-Self is already decided. Everything is Not-Self, *anattā*. On the one side stands I; on the other the whole gigantic cosmos, the duration, orgination and dissolution of which I recognize in and through my personality.

Because thinking is fully engaged by the Thirsting Will, it is incessantly irritated by this will. The Buddha says of such thinking that it is dirtied and begrimed by greed, hatred and delusion—the qualities of thirst. To denote this state of the thinking spirit we use the term "Mind". Thus those *saṅkhārā* of the fourth Group of Grasping may also be called the "creative" or "productive" activities of mind.

Of a vitally different nature is that thinking of the fifth Group of Grasping called *cognition*. This is "pure cognizing", no longer producing in order to satisfy a Thirsting Will, but confronting the total machinery of personality and also the Thirsting Will itself. Inspired by the newly awakened "will for *pure* cognition", it wants nothing else but to know.

The fact that such is the kind of thinking mentioned in the Fifth Group of Grasping, is stated explicitly in the following words of the Buddha: "Now there is left cognition (*viññāṇa*) alone, the perfectly pure kne, perfectly clarified one. With this cognition, one cognizes what? 'It is pleasant', 'it is unpleasant', 'it is neither pleasant nor unpleasant'." But whatever the nature of the sensation, the one who feels it recognizes that *it is produced* (*saṅkhata*). "And so he produces no more, thinks out nothing more, neither for the purpose that anything might

1. *Parenga* I, p. 114

be destroyed....This shows that he is no longer thirsting; because he is no longer thirsting, he will extinguish within himself."[1]

Hence, this cognition of the fifth Group of Grasping destroys the Thirsting Will and enables us to dispense with all that *creative* thinking of the fourth Group of Grasping serving for the satisfaction of the Thirsting Will and thereby with every conceivable kind of production. Thus the entire productive activity is finished forever. Therewith that activity of pure cognition reaches its final goal and, in consequence, goes to rest at the earliest possible date.

The Buddha calls this pure cognizing activity of the fifth Group of Grasping the meditative contemplation (*ñāṇadassana*).

As soon as the process of the originating of my personality and of the whole world is analysed, and every single component of this process itself is examined by the criterion for defining the boundary between the Self and Not-Self, it becomes clear that nothing of this belongs to my Self, but that everything lies outside it. For I stand behind the entire process and its constituent parts. In hours of contemplation and analysis I look down upon them as a cold, dispassionate spectator, as the pure subject of cognition. I observe their incessant arising and passing away, by which I myself, the observer, remain wholly untouched.

The Buddha deals in considerable detail with the body, pointing out that it must submit to the tyranny of decay and death. This inevitable cessation of the individual life affects all those productions which constitute what we call "being" peculiarly "man". The entire totality is dissolved by the nun Dhammadinnā, with the Buddha's explicit approval, as follows :

> "Three kinds of Productions are there—the corporeal, the linguistic and the mental. In-breathing and out-breathing is the corporeal Production, discursive thinking and reflecting is the linguistic Production, perception and sensation is the mental Production. In-breathing and out-breathing are corporeal faculties, bound up with the body. There-

1. *Majj. Nik.*, 140. Discourse

fore is in-breathing and out-breathing the corporeal Production. What one thinks conceptually and reflects upon, one utters in speech afterwards. Therefore is discursive thinking and reflecting the linguistic Production. Perception and sensation are mental faculties, bound up with the mind. Therefore is perception and sensation the mental Production."[1]

This definition of the productions is astonishing in its unsurpassed precision revealing the *kernel* of the matter. In-breathing and out-breathing is the basis and centre of the corporeal productions. The motion of life is to be regarded as starting from the process of breathing. Sensation and perception are the representatives of the productions appearing in the activities of sense. Conceptual thinking and reflecting form the kernel of the creative mental actions. Dḥammadinnā calls the third productions the linguistic *saṅkhārā* because the language serves the conceptional thinking—the reason—as its first product and at the same time its necessary tool. The contents of the fifth Group of Grasping is *meditative contemplation*, and therewith is already contained in the third Group of Grasping, perception.

The *saṅkhārā* of the fourth Group of Grasping are the creative mental actions, consisting in discursive thinking and reflecting.

The Buddha describes the opinion of a man regarding his future after death as a Production, whether a man believes he shall endure forever unchanged, or he perishes forever, or is uncertain as to what will become of him. The Buddha asks how such an opinion, whatever it might be, was engendered. He answers: "The ordinary man, not knowing the real matter of fact, has been hit by a sensation, originated in a contact taken place in the state of ignorance, and Thirst has arisen within him. From this comes the Production. Hence, thirst-born opinions are the productions. Opinions, however, are acts of thinking, and since these acts of thinking are called 'productions', they are productive acts of thinking.

It is now only too obvious why man is so helpless against the five groups which constitute personality. They all follow

1. *Majj. Nik.*, 44. Discourse.

their own laws. Even to-day, we are far from understanding adequately the laws governing our bodies. Sensations come and go against our will. Thoughts and moods vex us and we are helpless against them. We cannot expel them. How could all this be if they did, in fact, belong to our essence, if we consisted in them? What really and essentially belongs to us ought to be at our complete disposal.

Our volition could not possibly come into conflict with our faculties, because volition and the organs of its realization would be in the same degree essential to us. A faculty that was of our essence we would dominate absolutely, because our essence would set it in motion or suspend it when desired. Only that which is foreign to us has to be brought within our power. And this is exactly the case with the five groups which make up our personality. Most men cannot dominate them at all. Nobody can dominate them entirely, and only a trifling percentage even approach such a state. The few who gain a high degree of command, do so only as a result of incessant exercise and effort. It is a contradiction to assert our essence to consist in the elements of our personality and so in the personality itself.

The Buddha, who taught so much in allegory, pointed out that Warrior Kings had absolute power within their own domains, being able to destroy and preserve as they wished. He then pointed out that those who say, "Sensation is myself—Perception is myself—the Activities of my mind are myself—Cognition is myself", had to acknowledge that they had no or only very little dominion over these constituents of personality.

It is also true that, if we consisted of the five groups—if our essence were contained in them—then they ought to be to us the most natural and familiar thing in the world. They would be nothing but our Self, our I, and thereby completely recognized and defined. But, throughout his life, the individual regards and studies his body, sees it as a riddle, a mystery, as if it were something strange and novel to him. Not less does the man of reflective mind wonder at his faculties of sense, at the sensations, moods and thought arising within himself. He asks himself how he came into possession of his faculties, a question that would not be possible if he were nothing but the processes themselves. Were this the case, he would be comprehended in these processes, and more especially in the consciousness produced by them. This consciousness would be produced with the same machine-like self-evidence as steam is produced by the steam-engine. Consciousness and thereby man himself would be the adequate product of the conditions of their existence, would find their exhaustive and sufficient cause in them, and would without remainder be comprehended in them.

Whence then arises astonishment at consciousness and of the I-thought produced in it at their own existence and at the whole process producing them? But this astonishment exists. Nor is it mere astonishment of consciousness at itself. There is wonder that this consciousness is there—*a consciousness of consciousness*—of one who must be standing behind this consciousness. There is great wonder as to how the body, with its sensuality and consciousness, was acquired. How, for that matter, I ever got into this world.

The Buddha provided the answer to this mystery. Our rebirth is determined by the mode of the *thirst* pervading us, because this thirst leads to the seizing of a germ congenial to it. The task is to refine this thirst in order to transform it. And this is achieved by so shaping those creative mental actions that the transformation is accomplished. He who intends to form his next existence in a more favourable way and therewith settle after death in a world to which he may look forward, must cultivate, with an iron determination, those productive mental actions which will guide his Thirsting will in the desired direction.

> "If the man entangled in ignorance produces a productive mental activity leading to fortune, then his consciousness attains (after death) to a lucky world. If he produces a productive mental activity leading to misfortune, then his consciousness attains to an unlucky world. (This means: The universe to be experienced by him after death in his new consciousness—presents itself as a lucky world.) If he produces a productive mental activity directed upon freedom from disturbance (by objects of sense), then his consciousness attains to a world free from disturbance (Brahma-world)."

The Buddha makes it clear that everything depends on our mode of thinking. "From thinking all things have their start, by thinking they are directed, by thinking they are created. Him, who speaks or acts according to perverse thinking, follows Suffering like the wheel follows the draught-animal's hoof. In thinking have all things their root, by thinking they are directed, by thinking they are created. Him who speaks or acts according to pure thinking, follows well-being like the shadow follows him."[1]

"Whatsoever there are of unwelcome things: at first arises the thought about them, and the unwholesome things are subsequent to it. Whatsoever there are of wholesome things: at first arises the thought about them, and the wholesome things are subsequent to it."[2]

The organ of thought is the centre of all activities of the senses. Thus thinking is the Commander-in-Chief of all the productions which constitute the personality. The five outer organs of sense are simply the executive organs of this Commander-in-Chief.

It has already been noted that each being is himself the demiurge of his world. He creates the same again and again in the production of his corporeal organism through which alone we enter into our world and experience it. This will now be fully intelligible to us in all its aspects. We are such professional demiurges that we never rest from this creative activity. No sooner have we created a new world by our birth than we immediately begin to suggest to our world-constructor (our Thirsting Will for life), the plan for our next world. We do this in our present productive activities of mind; Mind in the sense of that thinking imbued with thirst.

This thirst leads us, at the moment of the dissolution of our present body, to the seizing of a quite distinct germ in a new mother's womb. The seizure is determined by our past mental activities. This germ we then form, by our Productions as the obedient journeymen of the constructor, into a new corporeal organism in which we enter into our new world.

Personality is nothing but a "heap of productions" (*saṅkhārā*).

1. *Dhammapada* 1.
2. *Aṅg. Nik.* No. 6, 6, 7.

These are of three kinds. The purely corporeal; that is, the activities of the several bodily organs; the functions of the senses, upon which sensation and perception are based; and the action of reason, consisting of deliberation and consideration. The action of reason—to wit, abstract thinking—together with the respective product of consciousness, we call mental processes. It is thought that the body, with its brain and organs of sense, does not constitute a sufficient substratum for man's mental or spiritual processes, and so a special substratum is postulated for them. Thus we are told of the "spirit", the spiritual substance which is said to be hidden as a special and separate something which furnishes the substratum for these spiritual functions.

The Buddha, with genius-like elucidation, explained that all the so-called spiritual functions, the functions of the senses in the proper sense, as well as those of mind and reason, are simply functions of the senses, including the functions of the organ of thought, effecting the arising of consciousness. The assumption of a spiritual substance or of a 'spirit' or 'soul', is nothing more than a hypostasis of those so-called spiritual functions themselves. It is the same tendency of the human mind towards personification which causes a native of the South Sea Islands who sees a motor-car for the first time, to suppose that a "spirit" within the machine gives it life. This same process causes men, when they do not understand the inner operations of any phenomenon, to substitute for the purely natural connection not yet accessible to him an independent force he supposes exists solely for this special purpose.

This assumption of a spiritual force, or, more precisely, an actual "spirit," disposes of all vexing problems in the simplest and most exhaustive manner. Guided by the Buddha, however, our investigations yield us the insight that man no more conceals a spirit within himself than woods hide dryads. There is nothing more at the base of spiritual notions and spiritual substance than purely sensual processes. The mysterious "spirit" in man reveals itself as merely a simple collective term for the so-called mental or spiritual functions, as distinct from the corporeal ones.

To understand the superfluity and untenability of the postulate of a particular spiritual substance, or soul, as bearer of the mental functions, it is only necessary to consider the following. If a separate spiritual substance exercised the functions of seeing, hearing, smelling tasting, touching and thinking, it would be able to use these senses interchangeably. That is, see with the ears, or taste with the eyes. It would be able to do this because it would hear and see by force of *its own essence*. In fact, if cognizing took place only in the soul, then the organs of sense would only prove a hindrance, in the same way that a keen-sighted man would find his sight hindered if he wore spectacles. But in reality it is just the reverse. The various psychical processes are exclusively bound up with the respective corporeal organs, the organ of thought included. The act of cognition is exclusively the product of the organs of sense, and not that of an entirely superfluous soul standing behind them.

There are those who maintain the existence of a soul who say : "It is true, the functions of cognition are bound up with the organs of the senses, the organ of thought included, but they are merely tools of which the soul makes use." Whoever advances such an objection forgets the principle that explanations must not be multiplied needlessly. If the organs of sense form the necessary presupposition of every act of cognition there is no reason why they should not form its *only* condition. This being so, one faces the following alternative : Either the assumed spiritual substance, or soul, must perish in death, since, having lost its material organs of sense it has used hitherto, it is no longer capable of cognition. If this is so, then precisely that is wanting which it was postulated to explain, and which forms its essential content; a soul which, together with its sensual activity, has lost all activity of mind and reason, is no soul, is, in fact, nothing at all. Or else the soul is able to carry out its cognizing functions after death when deprived of the formerly necessary corporeal organs. In this case, it is puzzling as to why it cannot effect in life, when its sense organs are only impaired, what it may do after death, when it is altogether without them. Thus, the concept of a separate "spirit", in common with every product of phantasy, breaks down before reality. Thus the Buddha describes the dogma of the self being constant and immutable in the form of an individual soul, "an utterly foolish idea."[1]

1. *Majj. Nik.*, 22 Discourse.

Although the untenability of the soul-hypothesis is manifest in every direction, men hold so tenaciously to the hypothesis as to show themselves inaccessible to every other teaching. But this is easy to understand. The average man identifies his essence with the five components of his personality, convinced that these components must stand in some essential relation to his real Self. Thus he lives under the delusion that it is his essence which manifests itself in his personality and presents itself as such. "The uninstructed man of the world looks upon body, sensation, perception, mentation and consciousness as himself; or he looks upon himself as possessing body, sensation, perception, mentation, consciousness as being in himself; or else he regards himself as being in body, sensation, perception, mentation, consciousness."[1]

For the mutation of the Thirsting Will, a series of existences, even world-periods, might be needed. "... the monk has to consider his mind, by uncovering it, often and often again. For a long time this Mind has been soiled by greed, by hatred, by perverse thinking. By the defilement of mind, the beings themselves are soiled, and by the purification of the mind the beings themselves are getting pure ...... the world-man not knowing the real matter of fact creates again and again a new corporeal form, creates again and again a new sensation, new perception, new productive activities of the mind, new consciousness".

"In dependence on ignorance arise the *Saṅkhārā*", the productions. With this we reach the last link in the formula of causal nexus, in its amplified form. From this placing of ignorance as the extreme end of the chain of causality we may judge it to be of fundamental importance. And so, indeed, it is.

It is clear that in this dictum the Buddha wishes to say that the productions are the outcome of an ignorance of something, *and would not come about if this something were known.* What might this something be ?

Firstly, as a practical ignorance there arises in man an immense fear of death, as he supposes it annihilates his ess-

1. *Majj. Nik.*, 109 Discourse.

ence. The reverse side of this fear is his boundless attachment to life, that is, to the Five Groups in action. This attachment usually maintains itself in the face of suffering, and to such an extent that men will even accept a life consisting only of suffering, if only they may be allowed to live at all, and this delays their supposed annihilation as long as possible. Here we come upon what is the deepest and last cause of this boundless attachment to life. This cannot reside in life itself being something worth desiring. It consists in the delusion that our essence is contained in the five groups of personality, and thus is doomed to destruction together with them. Persuade a man that sickness and death cannot touch him in his real essence, and he will at once regard them with indifference !

In addition to the fear of death, the belief in personality begets another, a theoretical fear. In consequence of his erroneous belief that his essence consists in his personality, death presents itself to him as his own dissolution. But against this assumption his essence, being in contradiction with it, revolts. And so, in despair, he seeks for a way out of this conflict between his inner essence and his needless apprehension of the relation in which he stands to his personality. Instead of seeing through this relationship, in a makeshift manner he reconciles his false apprehension with himself through a fresh error. He deceives himself into believing in the continued existence of his personality after death, in spite of the *obvious* fact of its annihilation. This error consists in the assumption of a soul. By making this assumption he is enabled to believe that his spiritual functions remain untouched by death since the soul is not subject to death. To be sure, the fact that the body finally perishes, cannot be explained away even by the assumption of a soul. But, because he detests the idea of going without his body forever, he imagines this body will be placed at his disposal, sooner or later, by the act of his almighty god. In such a manner, he masters all his difficulties.

Our real essence is as little impaired by this decay than is the body when it gives off odour. That is why the Buddha could exhort his followers to relinquish the five groups that make up personality with perfect tranquility of mind: "...what is not yours, that surrender ! Long will its surrender make for your happiness and well being. And what is it that is not yours ?

Body is not yours; sensation is not yours; perception is not yours; the activities of the mind are not yours; consciousness is not yours. Give them up, one and all! Long will their giving up tend to your happiness and well-being."[1]

But if the whole of personality, including all mental functions and the thinking and consciousness resulting from it, is dissolved in death, and behind this dissolved personality no substance or soul of any kind remains? What then of the individual?

This is the most crucial of all questions. We must reach the answer the Buddha gives to it by gradually coming to the point where the indirect path by which he has so far led us, namely that of pointing out to us wherein we do *not* consist, can no longer be followed.

For nothing more seems to remain over wherein man might erroneously find his essence, and so we ought soon to come upon the *positive* kernel of our essence.

In the first of the four most excellent truths we learn what suffering is. It is transitoriness, to which everything is subject, so that the whole world is one great world of suffering. Ultimately, there is the inevitable collapse of all the enjoyments and satisfactions of every kind, even the highest and most ideal. Man makes unceasing use of the organs of sense, because he fails to recognize, in accordance with truth, the consequences of these activities. Hence ignorance is the *basis* of the whole chain of suffering. It is the deep night, wrapped in which beings from beginningless time have used their six-senses-machine, with the result that, ever and again, new thirst for more of such activity arises. This thirst, in its turn, when the six-senses-apparatus breaks up in death, effects the constant upbuilding anew of the same. "Ignorance is the deep night, wherein we here are so long circling round."[2] According to this, it is established beyond all doubt that thirst is *conditioned* as the immediate cause of the circle of rebirth and thereby is a purely physical phenomenon. Even more important, *its final fundamental conditioning is recognized as being something, the removal of which is entirely in our power*. If ignorance is abolished, thirst and, with

1. *Saṁ. Nik.*, XXII, 29-33.
2. *Sutta-Nipāta*, v. 730.

it, all causality is uprooted forever. "Those who have vanquished delusion and broken through the dense darkness, will wander no more : *Causality exists no more for them.*"[1]

With this, we know the whole formula of origination through interdependence, and may well have seen that, in all its parts, it is lucid to the utmost degree. With logical necessity one link hooks into another, the whole chain of conditionings being both correct and exhaustive. In particular it has been shown to us that ignorance, as well as the Saṅkhārā, join on harmoniously to the conclusion of the formula treated above, which had the "corporeal organism together with consciousness" for its final link. Neither of them go beyond this last link, this being impossible according to the foregoing. For together with it, especially together with the corporeal organism which begins to take form at the moment of conception, there is given immediate linking up with the *former* "body endowed with consciousness" that had immediately preceded conception. So "ignorance" gives us the key to the understanding of how we have come to shape the germ, seized in consequence of our former thirst in a maternal womb, into a six-sense-machine and to make use of this machine.

The whole formula in its totality runs as follows :

"In dependence on ignorance arise the productions," building up the germ grasping in the womb into an apparatus of perception. In dependence on the productions arises consciousness. In dependence on consciousness arises the corporeal organism. In dependence on the corporeal organism arise the six organs of sense. In dependence on the six organs of sense arises contact. In dependence on contact arises sensation. In dependence on sensation arises thirst. In dependence on thirst arises grasping. In dependence on grasping arises Becoming. In dependence on Becoming arises birth. In dependence on birth arise old age, death, sorrow, lamentation, pain, grief and despair. Thus comes about the arising of this entire sum of Suffering."[2]

Until now, the understanding of this formula has been made so difficult because it was generally thought to be an

1. *Itivuttaka*, 14.
2. *Udāna*, 1, 3.

exposition of several links of the causal nexus in their *temporal* sequence. But the correct train of thought of the formula, and thereby the key to its understanding, is rather as follows: The Buddha wishes to show the relation of the single links in a purely *abstract* manner, in the way in which they condition themselves internally and in themselves, in the following manner: Old age and death, sorrow and affliction, pain, grief and despair are only possible in and with a body, as six-senses-machine. Such an organism must be born, therefore it presupposes birth Birth, however, is simply a special case of *Becoming*. Every Becoming is conditioned by a *grasping* and grasping is conditioned by the *thirst* for Becoming. Such thirst can appear only where there is *sensation*. But sensation presupposes organs of sense, which presuppose a *corporeal* organism for their existence. Such an organism can only exist if consciousness is added to it. But consciousness presupposes the building-up of the germ grasped by us into a six-senses-machine by means of the creative (productive) activities. *But these are only set going where ignorance exists as to the unwholesomeness of their results.*

These results, as the Buddha so often said, are "old age and death, sorrow, lamentation, pain, grief and despair."[1] And it is ignorance which is the immediate cause of the thirst for existence, which ever and again gushes forth anew from sensation.

Inevitably, the Buddha was greatly concerned to explain what is and what is not. He might have said: "You wish to be *something*, which probably means you do not wish to be *nothing*. But what is opposed to Nothing as its contrary? Obviously Everything. These are the most extreme and comprehensive opposites. Whoever is something is a part of everything. But what is everything? It is the eye and forms, the ear and sounds, the nose and odours, the tongue and flavours, the body and objects of touch, thinking and ideas. This is called Everything. But I have already demonstrated that you cannot consist in anything of this. And behind Everything there is only Nothing. Consequently, you are no Something. You are indeed—Nothing."

1. *Saṁ. Nik.*, XII, 44.

So then, it seems, I am fully summed up in the five groups constituting my personality, behind which yawns Nothing! I am nothing but this personality; and personality is nothing but a number of transitory processes without any abiding kernel. Accordingly, with the dissolution of this personality in death, I completely come to an end. Why then all these discussions about what I am not, if at last I am nothing at all. If this is the entire wisdom of the Buddha, he might have presented it in a much simpler manner. A later disciple of the Buddha, Nāgasena, explicitly declared that we are fundamentally nothing but a mere name, the foundations of which at death scatter to the winds. He said: "....there is no individual to be found." Faced with this assertion, Milinda, the king, replied: ".... if there is no individual to be found, who is it applies himself to meditation, realizes the Path, the Fruits, and Nibbāṇa? Who is it destroys life? Who is it takes what is not given him? Who is it commits immorality? ....In that case, there is no merit; there is no demerit. There is no one who does or causes to be done meritorious or demeritorious deeds; neither good nor evil deeds can have any fruit or result."

Nāgasena declared that a man is merely the sum of all his parts, in the same way that a chariot is the sum of all its parts. Disperse and burn the parts of a chariot and nothing remains. So with a man. When death takes over and the parts are no longer coordinated, then all is gone and all is finished. In fact, many have cited this dialogue between Nāgasena and Milinda as indicating that the Buddha's doctrine is the absolute annihilation of man. Are they right? This fundamental, primordial fact remains: Even if I see in regard to everything in the world that it cannot be my essence, that I cannot consist in anything within the world, *I am.*

It is because I am ignorant "in respect of corporeality" as of something fraught with suffering, that I continually use my six senses, with the immediate consequence that *as soon* as I use them, ever new sensations arise, and therewith thirst immediately makes its presence known. The ignorance, as cause, and thirst as effect, thereby meet in the act of sensation. Hence they do not lie apart in time. This being the case, if thirst is to be modified or annihilated, this is only possible by applying the lever to the primary cause of the activities of the senses—namely, to Ignorance.

The Buddha has pointed out "how ever and again a new personality arises", and thereby suffering is perpetuated. Precisely thereby he has also made available the key by which can be prevented the arising of a new being or a new corporeal organism, and thereby of a new personality. Thus he has shown the way to break through the chain of suffering, that one might break out forever from the circle of rebirths. To be enamoured and to shun are the two fundamental directions of *Thirst.* And thirst is the direct consequence of the activity of the senses. As soon as this latter sets in, in that same moment there comes about sensation and perception, and therewith also thirst.

Ignorance is, "Being void of Recollectedness as respects corporeality, bounded and limited of mind." But, "Knowing naught, in accord with truth, of the Deliverance of the mind, the Deliverance by wisdom, thereby all that is evil and insalutary, totally ceases to be," is meant a knowledge the individual does not possess and about which he does not exert himself. It is precisely this whole attitude of mind which determines his sense-activity. Only grasping bound up with delight is a grasping in the Buddha's sense of the word. The saint still satisfies his hunger and thirst, but not as a pleasure. Only as a necessity.

Upon every grasping there immediately follows a Becoming. As soon as I grasp, something becomes. At the moment I no longer grasp, for me nothing more becomes. But this is not the Becoming the Buddha means here. The Becoming here referred to is of a *new personality,* of a new existence which begins with conception. The ignorant man spends his *whole* life from his youth to his death practising grasping in all its forms. This grasping, which he indulges right until the moment of death, effectuates itself in a new germ just at the death-moment, and so brings about the becoming of a new personality. "In dependence upon Becoming arises Birth." This Becoming is brought about by conception—Birth in the Buddha's sense—but not that Becoming which still, during life, arises in consequence of grasping. Precisely because of this, *right to the moment of his death,* man has it in his own hands to put a stop to Becoming, of taking on a new personality, since it suffices that in this last moment he has no more thirst for life and thereby possesses the assurance that he will grasp no more at any new germ.

CHAPTER 2

THE FINDING OF THE MARVEL

(Unrevealed Secrets of Buddha's Mystic Teachings)

> "Among beings there are some whose eyes are not quite covered with dust; they will perceive the truth."

In his *Geschichte der Indischen Philosophie**, Erich Frauwallner writes:

"... Critics falsely claim that Buddhism denies the existence of a soul, and that therefore salvation means merely extinction (Sanskrit: Nirvāṇam, Pāli: nibbāṇam), it leads to a finality in nothing .... In my view, if one had not been prejudiced beforehand by the fantastically embellished legends of a later period .... the question how early Buddhism viewed the Problem of the soul and of the true nature of salvation would from the very start have appeared in a different light."

Frauwallner goes on to point out that knowledge of the *Mahāyāna* texts was responsible for evoking those assumptions. He then adds :

"How does Buddhism regard the question of salvation? Attempts have been made to read the answer to this question from the word with which Buddhism describes salvation, namely from the term for extinction (*Nirvāṇam, P. nibbāṇam*). This word signifies the extinction of a flame, and salvation is unjustly compared to such an extinction. It was then mistakenly thought that just as a flame disappears with its extinction, so, too, is the liberated one brought to nought with redemption. But this line of reasoning rests on rather false assumptions. ... the kindling and extinction of a flame did not mean for the Indian

* *History of Indian Philosophy*, Vol. 1, (Otto Müller Verlag, Salzburg, 1953).

long ago an arising and passing away, but the fire already existing becomes cognizable and again invisible, and this is the reason why that description is used for the fate of the soul after death."

This is in accord with the text which says : "The soul (*jīva*) that has entered the body perishes, but is like fire after the fuel has been consumed. Just as the flame is no longer cognizable because the principle of fire (without abode and therefore difficult to grasp) has withdrawn into itself so too the soul, when it has left the body, finds itself in a state "resembling the fire-in-itself, yet is not cognized because it is ethereal." The Buddha's conception of salvation is only analogous with the extinction of a fire. Just as the path of the extinguished fire cannot be known, so it is impossible to indicate the path of the completely liberated ones who have penetrated beyond the fetters and flood of desires, and have attained eternal, unchangeable bliss. Extinction is in no way comparable to annihilation. There is a sphere of extinction (*nirvāṇadhātu*) into which the redeemed one enters : "There is an unborn, unoriginated, unmade, unformed. If there were not, there would be no way out for the born, the originated, the made and the formed."

The Buddha lays great stress on the mistake a man makes when he regards his earthly personality as his true self. This leads him to attach a particular value to this self and to everything connected with it. He clings to it, and thus creates conditions which fetter him to this existence, and lead him from rebirth to rebirth. If, on the other hand, he recognizes that all this is not his true self, and in reality does not touch him, the craving is extinguished, he turns away from everything earthly, the fetters binding him to existence are broken, and he attains salvation. For the Buddha, salvation takes place through our recognizing as not-self (*anātmā P. anattā*) all that is falsely regarded as the Self, and so detaching desire therefrom. He stated : "..all this corporeality, sensation, consciousness, these forms, and this knowledge are not mine, are not-I, are not my Self."

The doctrine of the Buddha rests on contemplative thought never losing connection with experience as conveyed through the senses. It rests on the kind of thinking known as 'knowing and seeing', a phrase frequently repeated in the canon. The Buddha propagated his doctrine according to Platonic dialectic methods, on the art of logical thought based on perception. This art of logical thought rooted in perception is practised to a degree by the Buddha and he describes it as the 'Road to the Absolute'. He defines it as, "... *concentration combined with energetic logical thought and reflection*... which is the road to the absolute—to truth—to the other shore—to the subtle—the unfading—the eternal—to peace, deathlessness .... to the final goal."

Logical thought works with conceptions in which the total of all possible experience of the senses is preserved. The material it uses is the perceptible world, and so it is limited to the perceptible world. What is not accessible to perception through the senses *does not lie within the realm of logical thought.* Conversely, the realm beyond the perceptible world lies outside the realm of logical thought.

There is, however, something which lies outside the realm of logical thought. This he describes as, "... the deep, hard to perceive, hard to discover, peaceful, sublime, *not lying within the realm of logical thought* (*atakkāvacara*), subtle, to be experienced only by the judicious." In *Itivuttaka* 43 the Buddha says : "There is something not born, not due to causes, not created, not brought forth." And it is this which, by concentration with energetic logical thought and reflection, passes beyond the world of sensation and thus beyond the world perceptible. *This is the Delivered One, the Tathāgata.*

Again and again the Buddha stresses that a Delivered One cannot be grasped by knowledge, that it transcends every possible conception and all the processes of logical thought. "No one may know the way of the Fully Delivered Ones who have crossed over the flood of sensual pleasures and have reached unshakeable wellbeing."[1]

A Perfected One has separated himself from *all* things. "He is unsullied by all things."[2] For us all things are enclosed in the five groups of grasping, and the Buddha states : "If one clings to the five groups of grasping, one is defined by them.

1. *Udāna*, VII, 10.
2. *Ṣutta-Nipāta*, v. 455.

If one cleaves not to them, one cannot be defined by them." But the idea of Being is a purely empiric conception, being drawn from sensational experience. Sāriputta rejects all attempts at definition. He will not have, 'A Perfected One *is* after death,' nor 'A Perfected One *is not* after death'. Equally, he rejects, 'A Perfected One is and is not after death', and 'A Perfected One neither is nor is not after death'. He does so because all such concepts mean thinking in terms of corporeality, and such terms cannot be applied to non-corporeality. And the Buddha states most explicitly that there is no way to define a Perfected One.

Having pointed out that the opposite of Everything is Nothing, the Buddha then directs attention to the fact that, lying behind all the activities of the senses and of thinking, there is something in this so-called nothing. This is that most self-evident of all things—the Self. For we know that our innermost essence does not consist in the six-sense-activities and in their correlates, so that the Self stands behind these. The Self does not consist in forms, sounds, odours, flavours, tangibles and ideas, and since these are all the components of the world, the Self is beyond them—it is beyond the universe, Or to express the fact in the spirit of the Buddha : Everything is not yourself—*the SELF*—"the whole world is *anattā*."[1]

The Buddha pointed out that the instructed, noble disciple becomes disgusted with the body and all its activities, with sensation and perception, and even with the activities of the mind and with cognition. He disassociates himself from them and he is freed from them. He is aware that he is free, and he knows : "Destroyed is (the possibility of) rebirth, lived to the end of the Holy life, done that what was to do, no longer have I anything in common with this order of things." And because he has effected this complete separation, he is beyond the reach of any kind of recognizance and, for this very reason, he is not to be defined by any conception whatever. This means that he is *atakkāvacara, not lying within the realm of logical thought*.

When asked to define the Perfected One, the Buddha replied with the allegory of the fire that has gone out and

1. *Sutta-Nipāta*, v. 455.

which has become unrecognizable and, by virtue of that fact, is entirely removed from logical thinking. He said : " . . . a Perfected One is deep, boundless, unfathomable like the great ocean."

The Buddha went to great pains to explain what a man was not. He stripped away thought and feeling, but left the 'Self' which, most obviously, existed, being present in some sense or other. This is the literal meaning of *anattā,* which does not mean "not a Self", but "not my Self", and so presupposes the same Self.

"What is transitory, is painful, what is painful, is *anattā,* what is *anattā,* is not mine, this am I not, this is not my Self."[1]

The essence of a thing is formed by that which may not be taken away from it without destroying it. Man is a reality, therefore an essence of man in the given sense must also exist. The question therefore can never be *if* there is such an 'I', such an *attā* or "Self", but only wherein it really consists. The Buddha expressly stated that the saint experiences himself as standing beyond the five groups that make up the material world, and so as standing beyond the world.

There have been few greater misinterpretations of any teaching than the false claim that Buddha taught that the ultimate for the individual is absolute nihilism. Day to day experience testifies that a man is not affected in his real essence by the perishing of his material body. The senses dim, but the 'Self' remains, being all the time the subject of suffering. The Buddha stated expressly that he did not see himself as " . . . consisting in the earthly element, the watery element, the fiery element, the windy element, the element of space, the element of consciousness."[2] He also stated, "I am nothing that is, *nothing belonging to this world.*"

Whatever we look at in the world, whether it is a grain of dust or the Earth itself, as soon as we make an attempt to lay hold of its essence, we find that it eludes us. The realm of essence is hidden from us by an impenetrable veil. This leads to the establishment of the fundamental truth : *That our faculty of cognition is not adapted to cognize realities in themselves, and, least of all, to cognize our own* Essence. This is due to the fact

1. *Saṁyutta Nikāya* XXXV, 1.
2. *Majj . Nik.*, 112 Discourse.

that what is innermost and primary in every reality is not cognition, but that this cognition comes forth from it as something secondary and external, after it has provided itself with corporeal attributes, and by them has come into contact with the attributes of other realities. The faculty of cognition is designed purely for the cognizing of the mutual relations of these attributes. Thus cognition is, as it were, a light which only illumines a quite definite region amidst the boundless unlighted realm of origins within which it is lost.

Within the domain of the cognizable there is one fundamental axion which is absolutely irrefutable and which never can be shaken. On it, as upon a granite rock, rests the entire edifice of the Buddha's doctrine. It is the *Anattā*-idea which fixes, determines the fundamental relations between ourselves and everything cognizable. He expressed it in this Great Syllogism : "What I perceive to pass away within the framework of my personality and in consequence of this passing away, cause suffering to me cannot be my real essence. Now I perceive *everything* that is cognizable within the framework of my personality to pass away. . . therefore nothing cognizable is my real essence."

There is embedded in this cause for rejoicing. For the *Anattā*-idea creates the possibility of deliverance. As everything cognizable is not 'Self' therefore I can free myself from everything cognizable. To achieve this liberation, I must become selfless. In other words, I must seek nothing cognizable; nothing for myself at all. I may not relate anything to myself. But this I am able to do only if I learn how to *think* in accordance with highest reality. With a gaze thus alienated I must learn so to look upon the mechanism of my personality that in the course of this my activity of thought, "the inclinations of pride which think the thoughts 'I' and 'Me'[1] may arise no more." Instead, everything must meet me simply and solely as *an object* : a method of thinking which finds its classical expression in the *Paticca-Samuppāda*.

It is, of course, I who thinks in this entirely impersonal manner. And this kind of thinking is the greatest art I have to learn. I must dismiss the thought of all objects as having relation to myself. Far more, I must dismiss the Thought of

1. ahaṅkāra-mamaṅkāra-mānānuśaya.

myself, and the thought that there can exist anything belonging to me. "This does not belong to me; this am I not; this is *not* my Self." This kind of thinking must be practised to realize the further truth : "What exists, what has become, shall not be, shall not be there present *for me*; shall not become, shall not become for me; I let it go."[1] For when I am able to achieve the culminating point of selflessness in thinking, to think everything stripped of any positive relation to myself, I become entirely clear that, basically, I have nothing whatever to do with it. When this is understood, then the whole Canon will become as an ocean of light for me. Then deliverance will become easy for me.

"Mistaken attempts have been made to prove that the Buddha denied the existence of the Self. But the texts of the Buddhist Canon never say that a Self does not exist, but at most that it is not conceivable. It has also been claimed that the Buddha chose this method of expression in order not to alarm his weaker disciples who would have been shocked to learn that annihilation was the concomitant of salvation. But such devious trains of thought are quite alien to the Buddha's simplicity and directness of reasoning. Nor did he go in search of followers. He stated : "A denier is the ascetic Gautama, that he teaches the destruction, annihilation, and perishing of the being, that now exists. Only one thing do I teach, now as before, namely suffering and the abolition of suffering.

The Buddha declines to answer the question concerning the existence of a self, because he regards it as one of those problems which lead to barren discussion and explanation, and divert us from the only goal that—that of salvation. But a denial of the soul is not expressed; rather it is described merely as inconceivable, whereever an express statement occours."[2]

The famous sermon on the not-self expressly states that the Buddha makes it clear that none of the finite and fleeting elements of existence can be our 'self'. Thus it is expressly stated that there exists an ultimate absolute behind all fleeting factors. . . . A distinction is drawn between three kinds of the

1. *Majj. Nik.*, 106 Discourse.

2. E. Frauwallner, *History of Indian Philosophy*, Salzburg 1953.

(finite) self as possible (but erroneous) views, namely the physical self, the psychic self, and the self consisting only of contracts to consciousness. Man must be delivered from all three forms of the so-called self.... The pernicious peculiar to finite individual existence is in particular characterized by the assumption of the so-called ten fetters, the first five of which lead to a degenerate rebirth, and the rest (insofar as the first five are broken) to a higher existence which, of course, is also in need of liberation.

The Buddha expressly refuses to side with those ascetics and Brahmins who teach annihilation. In words of passionate protest the Buddha exclaims, "... many ascetics and Brahmins falsely, groundlessly, untruly, in defiance of fact, bring accusation thus : 'A nihilist is this ascetic Gautama. He preaches the cutting off, the destruction, the nullification of the present living being.' But.... these ascetics and Brahmins thus falsely, groundlessly, untruly, in defiance of fact, impeach me. For, as before, so also now, I preach only Suffering and the cessation of Suffering."[1] Defining the type of annihilation he teaches, the Buddha says : "I teach the annihilation of craving, the annihilation of hatred, the annihilation of delusion, I teach the annihilation of manifold evils that do not pertain to salvation."

Sāriputta, the greatest of the Buddha's disciples, said : "The learned and noble disciple conceives an aversion for the corporeal form, for sensation, for the activities of the mind and for cognition. And in conceiving this aversion he becomes divested of the influences, and by the absence of the influences he becomes free; and when he is free, he becomes aware that he is free." The Self is thus seen as wholly distinct from all physical and mental processes, and as something, in fact, that, without salvation, remains in bondage to them. But it is the physical and mental processes which terminate, not the Self.

The sages of ancient India concentrated upon finding out the fundamental principle which underlies all existence. This, they concluded, exists only within ourselves, for it is only within himself that each may plumb the deepest depths. In this search the men of ancient India reached the insight that

1. *Majj. Nik.*, 22 Discourse.

this fundamental principle is a man's own Self—the Ātman. They who desire to find the ultimate must search for this Ātman. And, from the outset, the conception of the Ātman was connected with the interpretation of the Self "as opposed to what is not Self." The Ātman, essentially and originally, is a relative concept, inasmuch as we always think of something that is not the Ātman. And it is a negative concept, in as much as its positive content does not consist in Itself, but in what is thereby excluded. Such limiting concepts have often been used by philosophers with great advantage, to designate the incognizable principle of things by excluding from it the whole content of the cognizable world. In this category is the "essentially existing" of Plato, as opposed to the arising and passing away; the "substance" of Spinoza, as opposed to the modes of existing, and also the "thing-in-itself" of Kant, as opposed to the whole world of phenomena. All these concepts are negative. They only tell us what is not, but it is precisely in that fact that there is to be found their value for metaphysics, which has to deal with something which is forever incognizable. Of such a kind is the concept of Ātman, which exhorts us to look at the essence behind our personality, and to put away everything that does not in a strict sense belong to this Self. It is the most abstract and therefore the best name ever devised by philosophy for its one eternal theme, as this alone goes to the point where the inner, dark, never appearing essence opens out to us.

In the Taittirīya-Upaniṣad man is presented, initially, in his external bodily appearance, which is described as only a wrapping. If this is removed, we reach the life-breathing self, which is merely a second wrapping. This is removed in order to arrive at the mind-self, and this is penetrated to reach the cognition-like self. This brings the seeker to the centre. But this cannot be entered or penetrated. Indeed, the seeker is warned not to make this ultimate interior of nature an object of cognition. But the point is made that the Buddha unquestionably assumed an ultimate Self about which he did not speak.

The Buddha taught in ancient India, doing so at a time when the country was imbued with a profoundly metaphysical spirit. "Here religions, outwardly most different, *join hands in the incessant demand to dispise as perishable everything earthly,* and to keep one's eyes on the imperishable, whether this be called Brahman, Nirvāṇa or anything else." It is freedom from the perishable—detachment from the personality and its world—which is the ultimate goal.

George Grimm points out that the Buddha's simple ideas, which could be understood even by a cowherd and appear again and again as the foundation of his teaching, can be presented in what he calls the 'Great Syllogism.' "This syllogism makes it obvious that one starts from justifiable data, which is always one's personality and that which is known thereby. Insofar as it is detected to be 'not the self', it is abandoned; and such is always the case in practical life. The presentation of this ancient wisdom was precise; it gave a thorough prescription for deliverance and enlightenment."[1]

As long as we adhere to the five groups they are qualities which belong to us, but they are not essential qualities. They have nothing to do with our real essence. This means that, as long as I adhere to them I am, of course, not without them, but if I let them go, I am thereby not touched in my essence. The Buddha repeatedly taught that the corporeal form is transitory and that which is transitory is painful and what which is painful ceases and disappears. The sensation, perception, activities of the mind, cognition are transitory, and that which is transitory passes and perishes.

All names and forms of the world are based upon the *Ucchiṣṭa, that which remains,* if we take away all forms of the apparent world. The concept of *Ucchiṣṭa* is as negative and relative as that of Ātman, and is closely related to it. The hymn contains an exhortation to direct our attention to *that which remains* if we think everything cognizable away. That which remains is designated "the splendour within."

To the question, "What is the 'I', the Self ?" Prajāpati gives three answers. The first means that the Self is the body with its sensitive and vegetative functions and perishes with the body. The second means that the 'I' can be an active spirit, released from the body. The third answer means spirituality wholly without any object, or, spirituality in its complete

1. Max Hoppe in Saher's *Evolution und Gottesidee* ; see also *Eastern Wisdom and Western Thought*, George Allen and Unwin, London 1969.

quietude. This is the state said to be really suited to the Self, and so is the real Ātman. The Bṛhadāraṇyaka-Upaniṣad 4, 3, 19 says : "The mind hastens to that state where it becomes entirely quieted, feels no more desire and sees no more pictures in dreams. This is its essential form, wherein it is exalted above desire, is free from Ill-will and void of fear.... The mind, embraced by the cognition-like Self, has no more consciousness of what is internal or external. This is its essential form, wherein it is of satisfied desire, is itself its desire, is without desire and severed from griefs .... Then is the father no father, and the mother no mother, the worlds are no worlds, the gods no gods .... If then he is without sight, yet is he seeing, although he does not see, for to the (essentially) seeing one there is no interruption of seeing, but there is nothing second beside him, nothing other divided from him, that he might see."

Later, in Yoga, men learnt of a state of the Self that is still higher than even the perfect quieting of the mind, such as supervenes in deep sleep. In deep sleep, the extinction of the world's expanse takes place unconsciously, and in such a way that cognition, too, is no longer its own object. But by means of the methodically exercised concentration perfected by Yoga, the liberation of cognition from the material organism and the extinction of the whole world's expanse, can be attained with *full consciousness*. By concentration one calls the five external senses 'home', so that one "no longer cognizes externally". All bodily functions, including inhalation and exhalation, are suspended, and the mind is fixed exclusively on the representation of boundless space. Then, by abandoning this representation, we bring the mind to the intuitive representation of how cognition itself is boundless. Thus we exist in our own *pure* cognition and cognize ourselves as "through and through consisting of cognition". Then we proceed to the intuitive representation of there being nothing any longer to cognize—the realm of nothingness—and, at last, by dismissing also this representation of nothingness from our mind, we rise to the highest representation. This is the realm of neither perceiving nor non-perceiving. This *conscious* state of purest objectless mentality is the very highest state of the Self, of the Ātman or the Turīyam : "Not cognizing internally, and not cognizing externally, also not consisting through and through of cognition, neither perceiving nor non-perceiving, invisible, intangible, incomprehensible, incharacterizable, unthinkable, indescribable, only *founded upon the certainty of the own Self*, extinguishing the whole expanse of the world, quisted, blissful, without a second—this is the fourth quarter (caturtha), this is the Ātman, that man should cognize."[1]

All this was thus *immediate experience*, direct cognition, and therefore stands firm beyond all doubt *in actuality*. The Self, the Ātman, is able to remain in these four states. On this *intuition*, produced by means of *reflection*, the *system* of the Vedānta was built up. It was said : If even during our lifetime it is possible to gain freedom from the body—in Turīya the body is a mass without sensation, by which we are no more touched—and to retire to pure and objectless mentality, then the death of a delivered one is nothing more than the *permanent* throwing away of the body, by *permanently* retiring to pure mentality.

The eternal and also blissful state of the Self seemed thereby to be discovered. But it was later concluded that, if the real Self is discovered, then thereby the real essence of the world must be revealed. For the essential nature of the world must be contained in everything existing in the world and in everything that exists. If a man *cognizes* himself, he also cognizes the ultimate, the primary cause of the world. In other words, the principle of the world must be identical with the principle of the Self. "As a piece of salt that has dissolved in water can no more be found, but must still be existent in the water, as the salty taste indicates, even so you do not perceive the existent here in the body, but nevertheless it is there. What this subtle is, of that this world consists : This is the real, this is the Self, this thou art (*tat tvam asi*), Śvetaketu."[2] From this, without break, followed the equilibrium of Ātman and Brahman, the principle of the world. And from this it ensued that this latter is to be defined as pure mentality, as the great, shoreless essence consisting only of cognition.

1. *Māṇḍūkya Upaniṣad* 7.
2. *Chāndogya-Upaniṣad*, 6, 13, 2.

To the saint, the process we call death is nothing more than the annihilation of those things which are, because they belong to this world, transitory, painful and produced, and which, therefore, do not form his real essence, his true Self. Only what is fundamentally alien to him comes to annihilation. This relationship is fundamentally misunderstood by the ignorant and unconverted. He brings the components of his personality into relation to his real essence, obstinately seeking them as if they were his Self. Precisely because he does this, he loses himself in his personality so completely as to be entirely absorbed into it. Hence he looks upon himself as doomed to death. The five components of personality become assassins bringing death to him. More especially do they become assassins of the state alone proper to us — the state in which there is freedom from these five groups —a state which, as we shall see later on, is one of ineffable peace. This thought of the components of personality acting as killers finds expression in the words: "Whoso does not taste of the insight into the body, truly does not taste the imperishable. He alone who tastes the insight into the body, truly tastes the imperishable."[1]

There are two sayings of the Buddha which may be quoted in which he solemnly announces the existence of the realm of freedom from suffering, the state which in truth is proper to us, and must therefore be looked upon as our real home : "There is something not born, not due to causes, not made, not produced by creative activity. If this something.... did not exist, then a getting out of this born, this due to causes, this made, this produced by creative activity could not be found. But because there is this something .... therefore a getting out of the born, the due to causes, the made, the produced by creative activity may be found."

"There is that realm where there is neither earth nor water, neither fire nor air, neither the realm of infinite space nor the realm of infinite consciousness, nor the realm of nothingness, nor the realm of neither perception nor yet non-perception, neither this world nor the other one, nor both, neither moon nor sun. This I call neither coming nor going, nor perishing nor originating. Without support, without progress, without basis in this, even this is the end of suffering."

1. *Aṅg. Nik.*, 1, 21.

Thus I exist, independent of my personality, and also after it is annihilated. This is the tremendous culmination of the doctrine of the Buddha, which may be gained on the basis of our own intuitive insight. It may be won by seeing through the realm of the Not-self; "Difficult to behold verily, is the Not-self", namely, in its quality as not our Self.

During the epic era of the Mahābhārata all philosophical and religious striving for insight was directed towards striving to uncover the real kernel of man. This was the case because this is obviously the right way, for it removed everything which showed itself not to be kernel-like or essential. At the same time they tried to penetrate to this kernel by means of Yoga, a method by which they sought to lay hold of this kernel or real Self. In this way they turned away from the outer world and tried to lose themselves ever more deeply in their innermost being by means of *Sāṁkhya*, by reflection. In this way they corrected the basic error of the Vedānta system, namely, the error considering the Ātman (the Self) and the world to be the same. They saw that, for pure objective cognition the totality of the objective apparent world, now called *Prakṛti*, is an independent factor opposed to the cognizing subject, and therefore is not merely Māyā. "One thing am I, and another is the *Prakṛti*."[1]

The Buddha also wanted to find the kernel of the human being, the *kernel*, the real and innermost essence, which cannot be separated from the Self, the Ātman (Attā in its Pāli form), by which word is most exactly designated the essential within us, and which, were it removed, would result in our annihilation. Inevitably, therefore, in the discourses of the Buddha everything circles round the Ātman. This *Attā* is the unchangeable centre to which all the discourses of the Buddha point. It is also the great problem in the doctrine of the Buddha. There is hardly a page in the doctrine of the Upaniṣads which does not mention the Ātman, nor is there more than the odd Discourse of the Buddha which does not deal with the Attā in some form or other.

The Buddha is also in harmony with the Upaniṣads and thereby with the general mode of Indian thinking, inasmuch as he

1. *Mahābhārata*, 11437.

sought to find the *Attā* by abstracting from it everything inessential to Self and which was separable from it. He even brought this method to its highest, classical Perfection by substituting for the basic question, "What is the *Ātman*?" the question, "What is not the Attā? What is Anattā?" By means of Sāṁkhya and Yoga, he solved the question definitively. He decided it in the following way : What can be separated from us without ourselves being touched at our core ? He went on to lay down the formula : What I observe to perish within the framework of my personality and with the setting in of this perishing, to bring suffering to me, cannot possibly be my Self, my Attā, but must certainly be Not-self, Anattā. This obviously infallible criterion he then used to investigate all the components of his personality, the body, sensation, perception, the activities of the mind and the cognizing faculty, and found them all to be transitory and thereby bringing suffering. By virtue of that fact they could not be his true essence, his Attā. He arrived at this conclusion by reflection and meditation, and he confirmed it by Yoga-practice. By this means, he did, in fact, separate himself from his body, his sensations, perceptions, mental activities and cognition. He did this by annihilating all perception and sensation (*saññāvedyatānirodha*). He then returned to the body to experience new sensations, new perceptions, new activities of the mind and new cognition. Thereby he obtained practical proof that the Self, the true Attā, is essentially different from all the elements of personality.

Everything recognizable in us was seen to be inessential, nirātman, anattā. Then how is the result of the Buddha's investigations to be interpreted, that everything is anattā, not my Self? To this must be given the observation of Einstein, "Interpret not, but acknowledge !" Acknowledge what is right beyond all doubt, whether or not we are able to digest its truth. If we cannot digest it; that is, cannot bring it into harmony with our world-view, this merely indicates that our current world-view is so false that a fundamental fact of reality cannot find room in it. That is what Einstein meant when said, "Interpret not, but acknowledge". To acknowledge means to ruthlessly accept all the consequences that follow from the discovered fact of reality. These are : If everything I can cognize within the framework of my personality is inessential to me, then I am able to separate myself from everything that is in any way cognizable, which means from everything transitory.

Radhakrishnan draws attention to both the burden and its bearer. "Nirvāṇa is not a lapse into a void, but only a negation of the flux and a positive return of the self to itself. The logical conclusion from this would be that something is, though it is not the empirical self. This is also in agreement with Buddha's statement that the self is neither the same as nor entirely different from the skandhas. It is not a mere composite of mind and body, nor is it the eternal substance, exempt from the vicissitudes of change. The discussion of the burden and its bearer makes out that the skandhas, which are the burden, and the pudgala, which is the bearer, are distinct entities. Were they identical there would be no need to distinguish between them. 'O ye mendicants, I am going to point out to you the burden as well as the carrier of the burden; he who holds that there is no soul is a man of false notions.' To be born is to take up the burden; to lay it down is to attain the bliss of Nirvāṇa."[1]

In his work, *Nirvāṇa*, De La Vallé-Poussin says : "When the Buddha refuses to endorse the identity of, or the difference between, the principles of life and of the body, he does so because the life-principle or life-essence is in fact neither identical with, nor different from, the elements. In comparison with the elements, the principle, essence, or pudgala is beyond description (*avācya*) ; the *pudgala* is not cognized independently of the elements, and hence it is not different from the elements. It does not have the constitution of the elements, for in that case it would be subject to birth and death; hence it is not identical with the elements .... It is also impossible to say that it is perishable or imperishable. The pudgala is like Kant's thing-in-itself (*dravya*) ; it is defined as the doer of deeds, and as the one who reaps the results thereof. Related to it are rebirth and nirvāṇa, the state of bondage and the state of freedom."

The Pudgala-vādins were in their heyday during the seventh century A.D. They were of considerable importance in the development of Buddhistic thought. Edward Conze says of

1. S. Radhakrishnan, *Indian Philosophy*, Vol. 1, pp. 386-387.

them : "They spoke of an indefinable principle called the *pudgala*, the person, who is neither different nor not different from the five Skandhas. It persists through the several lives of a being until he reaches Nirvāṇa. It has a sort of middle position between our true and our empirical self. On the one hand, it accounts for our sense of personal identity (like the "empirical self'), and on the other, it lasts into Nirvāṇa (like the 'true self'). Among all controversial issues, this one was considered as the most critical of all. Throughout the centuries the orthodox never wearied of piling argument upon argument to defeat this admission of a *Self* by the Pudgalavādins. But the more tenaciously and persistently one tries to keep something out of one's mind, or out of a system of thought, the more surely it will come in. The orthodox, in the end, were forced to admit the notion of a permanent ego, not openly, but in various disguises, hidden in particularly obscure and abstruse concepts . . . . As soon as the advice to disregard the individual self had hardened into the proposition that *there is no self*, such concessions to common-sense became quite inevitable."[1]

What happens when the individual has liberated himself from everything cognizable, if he, at his last death, has abandoned his body and with it all capacity for sensation conditioned by it, and thereby forever all possibility of becoming conscious? If this question could not be answered, there would still follow from it, as consequence, simply a further incognisable alongside the incognizability of our real essence, to be added to the other countless other incomprehensibles with which, in this world, we find ourselves confronted. There would follow, in fact, the incognizability of the condition into which we should be transferred at our last death.

This incognizability would also have to be taken into account as the necessary consequence of a fact of reality. But this condition, called by the Buddha Nibbāṇa, is indeed even in this life capable of being experienced.

In fact the Buddha speaks of the "seer of Nibbāṇa." It is cognizable that there all factors which might produce suffering in any way are absent, and that the Perfected One there will

1. Edward Conze, *Buddhism : its Essence and Development*, pp. 169-170.

be entirely without desire and thereby entirely happy. For what higher bliss can there be than not to be disquieted by any, not even by the slightest, unsatisfied wish ?

Another consequence of the incognizability of our real Self, our true Ātman is that the Self, separated from everything that in truth is not Self, is boundless and unlimited, since everything bounding and limiting the Self belongs to the realm of not-the-Self, of the cognizable. "Liberated from corporeality, a Perfected One is deep, immeasurable, unfathomable as the ocean."

But the most important practical consequence of the inability to cognize the real is this : As the real Self is entirely incognizable, then the question, "What am I ?" "What is the Attā?" is in principle meaningless, as the question presumes the Attā to lie within the realm of the cognizable and is therefore capable of being discovered. But it is basic to the teaching of the Buddha that our kernel, the Attā, cannot be grasped by means of cognition, and especially that it cannot consist in thought, nor be of the nature of cognition. He reached this conclusion because he found all cognition, and especially all thinking, to be conditioned by the organs of cognition which are obviously alien to us.

Thus the man who asks, "What am I ?" must land in a cul de sac. The right way to at least step out on a highway that might lead to our desired goal is to ask : "What am I not ? What is not my Self ?" In short, we must ask not, "What is the Attā ?" but "What is Anattā ?" This is clearly the only possible approach to this most important and subtle of all problems. As soon as anything cognizable inside or outside of me arouses even the merest thought of myself, then I have evidence that I have brought it into relation with myself and thereby to my will, whether in the form of inclination or disinclination. But if I am able to regard everything without exception, including my body, sensations and cognizing, exclusively from this point of view, "This I am *not*," then, in time, every kind of volition, everything *inessential* and *unsuited* to me, and thereby every kind of willing, must become extinguished and deliverance must ensue.

For these reasons the doctrine of the Buddha is called the doctrine of the Not-Self. But it is not called this because the Buddha denies the Attā, for it would be mad or meaningless to deny oneself, which is the primary fact which alone no one can doubt. For what is more real to any man than himself? To say, "I am absolutely nothing at all," is surely a dictum before which thinking recoils. For absolute nothingness neither denies nor affirms anything. The Buddha, in common with all great minds, sought for the Ātman. "Know thyself!" was the inscription on the temple of Pythia. And Heraclitus, in his search for his Self was able to assert that the boundaries of the soul could not be found, even if all roads were run through.

The Buddha also sought for the Attā in the *indirect* way. He removed from the Attā all that it is not. And he did this so thoroughly and with such success, that everything cognizable, and particularly the mental and the process of thinking, revealed itself to him as Anattā, as something that had to be overcome. He said: "You teach the Attā, but I only know what the Attā is not." There is an ultimate reality, and there is a point in ourselves at which we realise ultimate reality.

The modern form of saying "the Self is *transcendent*" is not the mode of expression used by the *Attā-vāda*, for whom it is not absolutely transcendent, inasmuch as it is found in pure cognition. It is really the language of the *Anattā-vāda*, for the statement "the Self is transcendent" means, "The Self is beyond all cognition. It can in no wise be found out." Said the Buddha: "I am not anywhere whatsoever, to any one whatsoever, in anything whatsoever." No kind of cognition penetrates to the Self, and therefore nothing at all can be told about it. The rest is—silence! And it is only this silence about the Self that the Buddha teaches. Beyond that he does not go. This is the true Ātman teaching, the true Attā-vāda.

In the Upaniṣads, which in their grandeur come nearest to the doctrine of the Buddha, our essence is defined as "being, bliss and thought." This is man's salvation. Smaller minds find the essence of man in his mental functions, and so they miss the great truths proclaimed by the Buddha and the claim made by Spinoza: "We feel and experience that we are eternal."

Those who assume that the essence of the individual consists in his mental functions, draw the further conclusion that the individual—puggala—perishes when the organs of thought break up. This explains the opposition between religion and science. Religion is unable to contest the scientific claim that even the highest mental functions are of a material kind, and so suffer annihilation in death. On the other hand, science cannot weaken the fundamental dogma of every religion of the indestructibility of the human essence, a dogma that has its roots in the super-rational conviction that we *feel* and *experience* that we are eternal.

Both sides are in error. Both sides claim that the essence of man must be sought in his mental qualities. Because this basis is *false,* there is no hope, at this time, of filling in the gulf deviding science and religion.

Here we encounter an immense difficulty. If it is an error to seek for the essence of man in his mental qualities and corporeal qualities, in what can man consist ? What remains if he is stripped of his physical, mental and conscious qualities and of his will ? Apparently, nothing. But who could claim, without being declared mad, that man consists in neither his corporeal nor mental qualities, and so consists of nothing at all ? Such a man would be inverting all words and conceptions, and transposing them to their contrary. What reasonable man would venture to do such a thing ?

There is one man who did just this. A man who declared to be unwholesome that has always been regarded as wholesome; who designated as ugly what has always been looked upon as beautiful; who defined as woe that which from all time has been called happiness. He even called *non-existing* that which man has always accepted as *existing*. And he elevated to the highest reality that which all men have always called nothing, and he declared it to be the highest reality in accordance with *actuality*. This man, of course, was Siddhārtha Gautama, known as the Buddha, the Enlightened One, who called himself the Buddha because he awakened from the dream of life to reality *as it is*.

In effect, he says : You wish to know your real essence. You think it self-evident that this your 'i' must consist of something which you *cognize* within yourself. Thus you come to designate the qualities with which you see yourself endowed as the substratum of the 'I', foremost being your perception, sensation and thinking. But what if your presupposition that you must consist of something cognizable were false ? What if there were something *incognizable* in you which is your real essence ? What further, in this incognizable, but real essence were above the laws of arising and passing away, and I could prove all this to you with compelling logic—nay, with palpable, visible evidence ? Of course, you think this incognizable to be contradictory in itself, as it is surely a contradiction to desire to discover something incognizable by means of cognition. But this is not what is meant. For the reality of this incognizable thing stands fixed from the very beginning as primary, pre-eminent fact. It is *your own* reality, the reality you call your Self, and is thus the most immediate fact of consciousness. The question is this: Can the cognitive faculty penetrate beneath into the depths of the individual's real essence ? In other words, how far does the light of cognition reach in the direction in which you are objectively absorbed ?

The Buddha deliberately evades making any positive statement as to the condition of the Perfect One after death; that is, after the personality has been cast off. Without exception he speaks of it only in negative terms, even teaching that in a true monk the thought of "I am" should never arise. This has been made the chief reason for imputing to the Buddha the monstrosity of teaching annihilation of the individual upon dying. This despite the fact that he repeatedly insisted that what perished in death are only the components of the Not-Self. The Buddha taught that, at death, the true man goes forth, entirely pure and liberated from all the stains of personality. He is beyond the world and in a realm forever inaccessible to knowledge. For knowledge he is nothing, but stress must be laid on the fact that he is nothing *only* for knowledge. Where the veil of nothingness sinks down upon knowledge, there every positive definition, even that of being, comes to an end. There is not even room left for the expression "I am" in its positive form.

In death, the holy one discards the six organs of sense and, with them, all seeing, hearing, smelling, tasting, touching and thinking. Accordingly it is senseless to declare him to be, simply because all being consists only in seeing, hearing, smelling, tasting, touching and thinking. But it would be just as wrong to declare the delivered saint *not* to be. Certainly, he no longer exists in the normal sense of the word, as he has ceased to see, hear, smell, touch, taste and think. Thus he has vanished as far as our powers of apprehension go, which are able to operate only in their natural sixfold direction. To the observer, he has become *nothing*. But this being, which alone is comprehensible for us, *is not being in itself*. It is only a certain kind of being. Just as our notion of Nothing is not an absolute, but only a relative nothing, only nothing for our understanding. But man mistakenly identifies himself wholly with that form of being which consists in the activities of the six senses. Because of this, he is accustomed to accept the notion of non-being, not in its correct sense as relative non-being, but in its absolute sense as absolute nothing. Instead of using the terms of nothing and non-being immanently, he uses them transcendentally. Thus he arrives at the false conclusion that, as being consists in the activities of the six senses, their cessation results in pure non-being, complete nothingness.

This erroneous conclusion is traceable to the human being finding himself so deeply enmeshed in sensory activities. Thus when he is confronted by something outside or beyond the compass of the senses, he can find no concept and consequently no word to fit it. The Buddha himself expounds this train of thought as follows:[1] We cannot in any way assert our true Self to consist in sensations. We cannot say that it is sentient because of its inner essence, as sensations themselves are conditioned through these sensual activities, and so only arise as something alien. After this, he speaks of the only possible remaining conclusion; namely, that our Self must be free from sensations. If we rid ourselves of sensation, it can no longer be said that the Self *is*. The apparatus of our faculty of apprehension is only adapted towards the external, towards the components of the Not-Self. Thus the faculty of apprehension is incapable of casting light upon the individual's essence.

"Outwards the Self-Existent bored the holes, therefore man may look outwards but not into the inner Self."[2] The same thought is expressed by Schopenhauer : "The I is the dark point in consciousness, as, on the retina it is exactly the en-

1. *Dīgha-Nikāya*, XV.
2. *Kāṭhaka-Upaniṣad* 4, 1.

trance point of the optic nerve that is blind, as the brain itself is quite insensitive, as the body of the sun itself is dark, and as our eye sees everything with the exception of itself. Our faculty of apprehension *is wholly directed outwards* . . . .Therefore everybody knows himself only as an individual . . . . *But if he were able to become conscious of what he is besides and apart from this, he would willingly let go his individuality and smile* at the tenacity of his adherence to it."[1]

If even the most all-embracing conception man is able to form, that of being, cannot be applied to our true essence, then every view pertaining to it is recognized as inapplicable and even impossible. "To say of a monk (already during lifetime inwardly) detached from his mind that he has the view : 'An Accomplished One is after death', or that he has the view: 'An Accomplished One is and is not after death', or that he has the view : 'Neither is nor is not an Accomplished One after death', all this is inapplicable. And why so? So far as a term reaches . . . so far as an explanation reaches, so far as a presentation reaches, so far as the way of a presentation reaches, so far as wisdom reaches, so far as the realm of wisdom reaches, so far as a circle extends, so far as a circle encircles : just so far the circle encircles." Thus it is not applicable to say that a monk released in such knowledge, no longer cognizes, no longer sees.

Of the redeemed one it cannot even be said, "He is", and still less can it be said, "He is something identical with himself." Neither is there anything within the world (personality, especially, is nothing of the kind) identical with the Self; nor yet may my true essence be defined as such. For the conception of identity, as abstracted from experience, presupposes a sequence of changes, and thereby at least a point in time wherein something shall be identical with itself. But in the redeemed one all change and all time have been done away. As long as he is alive there is present only the *appearance* because in his innermost depth he remains untouched by the succession of changes.

This becomes clear in death, when all time ceases, and from when onwards the very expression "to persist" has no meaning. Thereby it is established that even in his lifetime he cannot

1. Schopenhauer, *World as Will and Idea.*

have been a persisting being in the strict meaning of the term, death not having touched him, but only the component parts of his Not-Self. The concept of persistence or of identity is meaningless. The fact itself can only be correctly defined by such negative expressions as "changeless" and "deathless". Most acute, and quite in the sense of the Buddha, are Schelling's remarks on this point : "In so far as the I is eternal, it has no duration at all; for duration can only be thought of in relation to objects. We speak of the eternity of duration . . . of an existence lasting through all time, but eternity in its pure sense (*aeternita*) is existence *outside of time. The pure and original form of eternity lies within the I.*"

It is as impossible to determine accurately the boundaries of cognition from its own structure, as it is impossible to determine the strength of the eyes from a mere physiological examination of the eyes themselves. It is only by means of a *practical* test that the boundaries of cognition may be determined with any degree of certainty. But this method of determining the boundaries of our cognition is beset with immense difficulty. When it is a question of identifying a definite object, then at least one characteristic mark of it must be known. Otherwise there is the risk of a wrong object being taken as the one sought for. A man looking for gold must know at least one specific characteristic of gold. It is the same with the Self. At least one infallible characteristic must be known if I am to be able successfully to examine the objects of my cognition as to their identity with my Self, if I am to guard against the risk of taking something for my Self which in reality is not my Self.

Fortunately, the relation between the Self and the faculty of cognition is such that, in every case, this indispensible criterion may be obtained. This criterion, as much as the reality of our Self, is an immediate fact of experience. Precisely because it is such, it requires no proof. Indeed, it is incapable of proof.

In this manner the Buddha first fixed the special *object* which he wished to grasp, to comprehend, to embrace with his cognition. To grasp this object with the cognition he directed his power of knowing towards everything cognizable within his personality and around him. This searching process produced the following result : Cognizing is no simple process. Under close inspection it resolves itself into several elements, into sensation, perception and thought. In this process, the inner relationship between these elements is such that sensation originates first, followed by perception of the object senses, and then the subject thinks about the object.

What is called god — at least insofar as this god is internally experienced — is nothing more than our innermost essence. This fact becomes exceptionally clear in a reading of the Christian mystics. It is a fact which gives consonance to the words of Schopenhauer when he said : Of such a god we can have no other theology than that which Dionysius Areopagita gives in his *Theologia Mystica,* which consists merely in the explanation that about god all predicates may be denied, but not a single one may be affirmed, because he is beyond all being and all knowledge. Dionysius calls this 'the Beyond',— the Buddha speaking of the 'other shore' and describes it as something entirely inaccessible to our knowledge. This theology is the only true one, only it contains nothing at all. It expressly tells and teaches nothing, and consists only in the declaration that it knows this very well, and that it cannot be otherwise. This is supplemented by the words of Angelus Silesius :

"I am a blissful thing, a non-thing tho' I be;
To everything that is, 'tis an unknown mystery."

It is also underwritten by this passage from Merswin's *Book of the Nine Rocks* : "Tell me . . . how are these men called who have seen into their origin ? I will tell you. You must know that these men have lost their names and become nameless, forever removed from the ocean of this world."

"As far as the six realms of contact extend, just as far extends the expense of the world (*papañca*) ; and as far as the expense of the world extends, just as far do the six realms of contact extend. With the annihilation of the six realms of contact without a remainder and without leaving a trace behind, the expanse of the world is extinguished, the expanse of the world comes to rest."

Where nothing at all is sensed, nothing is perceived; and where nothing is perceived, nothing is thought, for want of any object upon which thought might act. "What one senses, that one perceives. What one perceives, that one thinks." According to this, upon still closer scrutiny, the process of cognizing dissolves into countless sensations, perceptions and thoughts which incessantly follow one another. This analysis, although it has been very summary, shows that the various sensations, perceptions and acts of thinking are not essential to us. Each human being has millions of such sensations, perceptions and thoughts, and all are scattered and gone. Nevertheless, the individual exists. The sensations, perceptions and thoughts of this moment, as with all those experienced in the future, will pass away without taking *me* with them.

This brings us to the principal question : I know that all my sensations, perceptions and thoughts are dependent on me, that they proceed from me, and are based on me. In short, I know that I am able to produce sensations, perceptions and thoughts. And it is this that we mean basically when we say that these three activities are *essential* to man. We wish to state thereby that ultimately we are not summed up in the various concrete sensations, perceptions and thoughts, but much more in the *capacity* of having such things, so that in every case, with the annihilation of this *capacity*, we ourselves ought to be annihilated.

It is demonstrable beyond all dispute that the individual does not consist in these activities of sense and mind. Every organ of sense, including the organ of thought, is material. Like the whole bodily organism itself, it represents a high-potential chemical combination of the four chief elements. As soon as organ of sense is stimulated by an external object it begins to vibrate, and so excites sensation. Later, perception of the object senses calls into existence thinking about it.

Now it is recognized that the four chief elements, which build up the whole apparatus of cognition as well as its several organs of cognition, can on no account have anything to do with my essence. I seize them as nourishment, and so I must have existed *before*. Further, in my real essence, I take no part in the incessant vibrations of the organs of cognition which produce the sensations and perceptions for me. Rather I behold the origination and annihilation of these vibrations. Further, I myself, untouched by all this, perceive the gradual wearing out of these organs of cognition and their ultimate decay, with the result that I experience sorrow, grief and suffering. Therefore, these organs of cognition and the entire apparatus of cognition, are wholly alien to me, and have nothing to do with my real Self. Thus it is estabilished that cognition is entirely objective, and that the entire *capacity* to feel, perceive and think is not an immediate and organ-less function of our essence itself, but that we possess this capacity only so long as we possess the organs of cognition, organs which are obviously alien to our essence.

If the capacity to feel, perceive and think is inessential to me, then this is much more the case with every *object* that I feel, perceive and think about by means of this capacity. Not even my will belongs to me in such a way that I should be annihilated were my will annihilated. For it is only a will for *objects* felt, perceived and thought, springing up ever anew in desire, repulsion, hatred, passion and so on. For wherever nothing is felt, nothing is wanted.

"In a Perfected One corporeality, sensation, perception, activities of the mind, this cognition would be extinguished, their root would be annihilated. The Perfected One is free from this . . . . *He is deep, immeasurable, unfathomable like the great ocean.* That a Perfected One exists beyond death does not apply; that a Perfected One does not exist beyond death does not apply; that a Perfected One neither exists nor does not exist beyond death, neither does this apply."[1] In fact, nothing in the world any longer applies. A Perfected One in his purity, rid of the dross of his personality, beyond death is something uncognizable and inscrutable.

In attaining this result, the firm ground that supports all our knowledge seems to crumble, just because it lies beyond the apprehensible. Nevertheless it indicates to us the direction in which the thing apprehended lies, the thing itself remaining veiled inasmuch as it cannot enter apprehension and so appears as nothing.

Because it appears to ordinary apprehension as nothing, there is no longer room left even for the mere thought of the 'I'. In spite of this, no thought arises in us more often than that of 'I'. Indeed, it accompanies all our thoughts as the logical 'I'. "I hear . . . ." "I see . . . ." and so on. Thus it is essential to become clear as to the origin and content of this thought of 'I' as it was to achieve clarity regarding the thought of *being*.

This is provided by the insight gained by the Perfected One, who enjoys the view of Anattā in its perfect purity. Having dismissed the entire outer world from his mind, he contem-

1. *Sam. Nik.*, XLIV, 1.

plates the origin and dissolution of the five groups of grasping thus : "Such is the body, such is the origin of the body, such is the dissolution of the body; such is sensation, such is the origin of sensation, such is the dissolution of sensation, such is perception, such is the origin of perception, such is the dissolution of perception; such are the activities of the mind, such is the dissolution of the activities of the mind ; such is cognition, such is the origin of cognition; such is the dissolution of cognition."[1] In such contemplation, where is there room for the 'I'. Seen in this way, the whole machinery of personality shows itself to be merely a whirl of processes, which to the spectator appear as something alien to his essence. In regarding them, the temptation to think in the form of 'I' and 'Mine' no longer arises. Instead, even in regard to his apprehending activity itself, the only thoughts aroused discharge themselves in the great formula : "This does not belong to me, this am I not, this is not myself."

The "uninstructed man of the world" feels himself to be so intimately interwoven with his personality that, as the Buddha says, ". . . the inclination to believe in personality adheres to him" to such an extent that he imagines himself to consist entirely in it. In observing the incessant originating and dissolving of the five groups, he imagines that he sees himself incessantly originating and dissolving. And so he says : "I originate, I dissolve, I feel, I perceive," and so on.

We arrive at the thought of our I only if we see ourselves bound up with the five groups of grasping—that is, bound up with our personality. We then lose ourselves in them, being incapable of opposing ourselves to them with estranged regard.

"What do you think, ye disciples : Is the body, sensation, perception, the activities of the mind and cognition—are they permanent oder transient?" "They are transient." "But what is transient, is this painful or pleasurable?" "I is painful."—"Now if we do not grasp what proves itself to be transient, painful, subject to all vicissitudes—may then this doctrine arise : This (personality as the totality of the five groups) is my I, this is the world, and this my I will become after my death—permanent, lasting, immutable'?" "Certainly not, O Lord."

1. *Aṅg. Nik.*, IV, 41.

With this we have caused everything knowable to pass before our cognizing power without recognizing anything of it as our 'I'. The true Self, therefore, is not to be discovered as an object of cognition. It does not enter into our consciousness in any way. It is transcendent. This being the case, how can we possibly know anything about it ? How are we able to ascertain the reality of our Self? And how can we establish the criterion for the identification of our Self by means of consciousness, if the Self makes no appearance in consciousness ?. Is not this a contradiction in itself ? It would be a contradiction, if what is here taught about our Self was based on the pretence of *immediate* perception of the Self. But this is the very opposite of the case. What we have heard about our Self so far has been gained solely from meditation of Not-Self. We have paid regard to the objects of this realm which alone are accessible to our cognition, in a certain direction ; namely, insofar as their relation to ourselves is concerned.

It is analogous to a driver with an electric reflector who is driving at night. He sees everything that comes within range of the reflector, *and he also recognizes it in relation to himself.* But he himself does not enter the light of the reflector because he is sitting behind it. In exactly the same way we are only able to recognize the objects of the realm of Not-Self, for these alone enter the realm of cognition, while we ourselves do not. For we are the subject of cognition *which underlies* all cognition, *and for which alone the light of cognition shines.* Also we are able to recognize every object of cognition *in its relations to ourselves*, as this represents a cognition of the object in a certain direction. There is, in fact, no Self-consciousness, but only a Not-Self-consciousness, only a consciousness of what is really *not* our Self, not our 'I'. This insight is voiced in the Bhagavadgītā, 11, 71 : "Who lets go all enjoyments of the senses, and wanders on without desire, without Self-Consciousness, and without selfishness, will gain peace." To teach us to think in this abnegatory manner about everything entering the realm of our cognition is the sole purpose of the Buddha's doctrine.

Thus the doctrine teaches us to think in *harmony with the highest reality*, in contrast to the ordinary thinking of all others who mistake something that really is not their Self for their Self.

As all qualities and processes are only qualities and processes within the realm of Not-Self, therefore all possible conceptions and words are only valid for this realm of Not-Self since they have been devised solely for these qualities and processes.

Thus the cognizable stands opposed to the incognizable, the physical to the metaphysical, since the "cognizable" and "physical" are, in the last analysis, identical conceptions. The incognizable am I, the cognizable is the world, to which belongs all that is cognizable in my personality—my feeling, perceiving and thinking. But if I am not summed up entirely in the physical world, then I, myself, am no part of that world. That being the case, I must be able to free myself from that world. What then, for me, will take the place of the world? Of course, nothing. For if we could say something would take the place of the world, the something would have to be cognizable and so of the world itself, for the notion 'something' is wholly abstracted from the realm of the world.

The Self, separate from the world, will be apart from it when the world has been overcome and left forever. It will then be confronted by nothing cognizable, because, at the last death, there is nothing cognizable and that whole apparatus of cognition is discarded for always. This reality was referred to by the Buddha when he said : "There is a not-born, a not-become, a not-created, a not-formed ... If there were not escape from the born, the become, the created, the formed could not be known." And of that which is beyond the last death he said : "There is yonder realm where there is neither earth nor water, neither fire nor air, neither the boundless realm of space nor the boundless realm of consciousness, neither this world nor another, neither moon nor sun. This I call neither coming nor going, neither origination nor annihilation. Without support, without beginning, without foundation is this. This same is the end of suffering."

The Buddha makes it plain that the I-idea is based upon a misunderstanding of our relation to our personality, having its origin in the fact that the psycho-physical process begins which we call personality and therewith, at the same time, the illusion originates that this process—which includes seeing and hearing, etcetera—is essential to the subjective and constitutes the action of its own *essence*. This delusion makes the subjective the "subject of inherence", and in so doing makes it the empirical and thereby the *logical* 'I'. Now we do not say, as in truth we ought to do, regarding all processes as alien to the 'I' : "There arise movements of breath, there arises a sensation, there arises a thought." Instead, we say, "I breathe, I feel, I think", meaning, "I am *essentially* a breathing being, a feeling being, a thinking being." And so the true Self, which really lies behind these processes, is at once regarded as consisting in them. The processes are thought to belong *essentially* to the Self. Thus we have the conceptual reflection of this wrong view, when the Self made the subject, and thus the bearer of the predicates so wrongly attributed to it. The Buddha is at considerable pains to show that the entire personality is as foreign to us as the trees of a forest.

The supra-mundaneness of the Self is clearly shown in the following : "The empty world, they say, Lord. But why do they say so?"—"Because the world is empty of the Self and of anything belonging to the Self, therefore they say, 'the empty world'.

Nevertheless, it remains true that I am bound to my ego, and that I am using the machine of the six senses and thereby producing consciousness. In this sense, as of attributes *not essential* to us, a Perfected One also may certainly think and say : "I possess this body, I feel", and so on. But at the culmination of pure insight he has overcome the form of thinking with the I as subject. He perceives that his being is coupled up with the components of his personality which are essentially foreign to him. For the rest, he realizes that his insight does not penetrate to his real Self. In those depths, inaccessible to apprehension, the *actuation* of the machine of the six senses also goes on.

Thus we cannot perceive how we put the heart, lungs or other organs in motion, nor even which nerves and muscles we use in hearing, seeing and thinking. The vegetative functions, like the sensitive ones, perform below the threshold of consciousness, the light of consciousness being limited to the machine already in activity. From this it follows that thinking neither troubles itself about the Self as such nor about its connections with personality, because it is unable directly to apprehend anything of them. It occupies itself solely with the material processes of personality, which alone may be apprehended. In fact, thinking that is entirely adapted to reality does not occupy itself with the *subject* of cognition, which is wholly inaccessible to the faculty of cognition, but only with the *objects* of this cognizing faculty which alone may be cognized. But even with these it only is concerned insofar as their relation to this subject of cognition may be determined *from themselves*, which determines that all these objects stand in no kind of *essential* relation to the Self. At this level of insight we may think : "This originates, this perishes; this shall originate, this shall perish."

That I am the one who is thinking and creating all this never occurs to consciousness as a self-evident fact, or at least only in the form of the *Anattā*-thought; only in the negative form that everything cognizable has nothing to do with my *essence*. We have no Self-consciousness. We have consciousness only of what is *not* our Self.

This perfectly objective thinking, strictly limiting itself to the *objects* of apprehension, in which reflection in no wise ventures beyond intuition, can only be cultivated in hours of meditative contemplation. A man who wishes to share his insight with others must think and speak in taking the 'I' as subject, if only to distinguish his experience from that of others. Thus did the Buddha. For the time of meditative contemplation he taught wholly objective thinking, but for the rest, the form of thinking having the 'I' for its subject, as far as this imperfect form of thinking is not contrary to Reality.

The Indo-Europeans who settled in India always called themselves Aryans. The original meaning of the word "ārya" is "devout", "pious", and so Aryans are "those belonging to the pious". "Pious" is a *religious* concept, and means having a religious view of life and the world. But a view of the world is religious when a man feels obliged to pay heed to the securing of his great future after death, and regards himself as "bound" (*religatur*) to this obligation, whether he believes in a personal god or not, This is the proper meaning of the concept "religious". On account of this obligation of his conscience, a religious man sees himself compelled no longer to arrange his conduct exclusively for the unrestrained satisfaction of the desire for sensual pleasure, but to ponder the consequences that might result for the coming life from such a brutal egoism. Thus a religious view of life leads to an ennoblement of man's conduct.

From the beginning, the Aryan Indians have been religiously minded, and remain so to the present time. They rank, in fact, as the most religious people on earth. For the Indians, reality is not material, as it is for the nations of Europe and America. For them, the greatest reality is that proclaimed by the Buddha, "The glory of Nibbāṇa". In this domain of Reality, or in the Absolute—*Paramatthasāro* nibbāṇam—Nibbāṇa is the highest reality". In this domain there is no more *multiplicity*, nor is there a *Unity* there, such as is taught by Pantheism and absolute Monism. These picture the absolute reality as an ocean out of which the individual being emerges, rather like steam rises out of the ocean. Later, these beings return to their ocean like drops of water in which they again dissolve.

The Buddha points out that those beings who as Perfected Holy Ones have rid themselves of all "attributes" (*upādhi*), through which alone they are sundered from the Absolute Reality, sink back again into the latter. Of such a Perfected One the Buddha says, "He is submerged in the Deathless". This Deathless is my home in which I am submerged. The Perfected One is "gone home", and "for he who has gone home there is no standard of measure."[1]

Such are the realistic metaphysics of the Buddha. This *science* of metaphysics is as exact and as certain in its results as is the science of physics. For these metaphysics have exactly the same things for the objects of their investigation—namely, the things of this cognizable; and they meditate these things after the same method as physics. That is, according to the methods of logic and direct experience. The only difference between them is *the point of view* from which they look at things. Physical science regards things in their relations one to another. True metaphysics regards the cognizable in its relation to the student, the seeker, the saint. In other words, to the Self.

The metaphysical is just as certain as the physical. In fact, it is such more certain, for it can no more be argued away than

1. *Sutta Nipāta* v. 1076.

my own essence can be argued away. For this same metaphysical I myself am, and it is the highest situation possible to me. This kind of metaphysics is only reached by means of a certain scientific meditation of *things cognizable*. Thus *these* metaphysics do not transgress the boundaries of cognition, nor do they dabble in imaginary worlds and their equally imaginary inhabitants, as pseudo-metaphysics are wont to do.

The metaphysics of the Buddha discover the completing portion of that part of reality that alone is known to us. Therefore, in the Buddha's doctrine of reality, the great contradictions between religion and science are resolved. To renounce the world becomes just as intelligible as to enjoy it. Indeed, to renounce it is recognized as wholesome and sublime. The fundamental dogma of every religion is the indestructibility of the human essence. Modern science teaches that everything in the world, including our entire personality, is subject to incessant change and ultimately to complete dissolution. Assuredly our essence cannot die, since everything that is mortal is not our essence. And so, their differences resolved by the doctrine of the Buddha, science, without contradicting itself, leads on to religion and religious feeling.

True cognizing is *direct* cognizing, consisting in the *immediate* perception of an object by means of our sense-organs. This direct cognizing taken by itself, knows nothing of concepts and words, of reflection, proofs and conclusions. Rather do these things represent expressions of another independent faculty called *reason*, which may be associated with direct cognition, although it is not forced to be so associated.

Every philosophical view of the world is based on two elements, namely a looking out into the external world, and a looking into one's own depths. With the Aryans looking inwards is the essential thing. The man who identifies himself wholly with his personality arrives at a radically different view of the world from that of the man who recognizes his personality as a mere "attribute" inessential to himself. The rishis, or wise seers, arrived at this latter knowledge. They knew themselves in their very core to be untouched by the decay of their body. They knew themselves to be immortal, and for them arose the problem of the nature of their future after death and how that future might be safeguarded.

From his own inner being the ancient Aryan deduced the true kernel of all the forces of nature. How correct this is, is gathered from the fact that only in ourselves can we descend into the ground of the world in which we are rooted. For everything manifesting itself to our external senses always reveals to us only its outer shell. Kant confirmed the Aryan deduction when he said : " . . . the concept we have generally of all substance *has been borrowed by us from this I or Self*. This is the original concept of substance." The Ṛṣihi Dīrghatamas who lived during the second half of the Ṛg-Veda period, said : "Diverse names the poets give to that which is only one".

In the well-known Hymn of Creation it is asked : "Who has perceived whence comes creation? From it the gods of this world have sprung. Who therefore states whence they have come?"

At this stage the answer was that there was placed on the throne a supreme God called Prajāpati, the "Lord of Creation". But he was still a person. Nevertheless, he differed from the personal God of Christianity in that he did not place the world outside himself. On the contrary, he transformed himself wholly or partially (that is, without detriment to his continued personal existence) in-to nature and the phenomena. "He over whom nothing higher exists and who has entered into all beings, Prajāpati, favouring himself with children." This view of the world determined man's goal and the morality needed for its realization. This goal was the attainment of the world-community, the complete community with the gods, and thus arrival at the true eternal home.

The pure, direct action of cognition is the highest kind of cognition. Why, then, do we not confine ourselves to this type of cognition ? Why bring into play at all the activity of reason ? We do so because we are often unable to fully *apprehend* any given object, and so we exercise reason in order to correct a defective understanding. We try to fill up the gaps in our apprehension with rational conclusions. The exercise of reason is also necessary when I am no longer a mere spectator of the world-drama, but become an active participant along with others. Then mere perception is not enough. I must look out for my future. But in order to determine the nature of my future and then be able to realise it, I must draw conclusions from perceived reality. I must draw conclusions regarding that which is not to be directly cognised, and is as yet unreal, although it is becoming real. For instance, if 'A' exists, then 'B' will come into existence. If 'A' does not exist, then 'B' will not come into existence. But in order to be able to draw conclusions, we have to translate our perceptions into concepts and words.

It is only by means of concepts, supported by memory and imagination, that a comparison of the innumerable separate phenomena as they present themselves to perception, becomes possible. But the forming of concepts in itself presupposes a sorting out of the innumerable objects perceived into classes, since every concept represents the subsumption of a particular class of single perceptions from a certain definite point of view. In consequence of this sorting out or classification, the Eternal How, which alone is known to the primary type of cognition—that is, to perception—is differentiated into past, present and future. At the same time, in the same way that individual phenomena are subsumed under concepts. These forms of thought, taking shape by gradual adaptation to perceived reality, produce in their totality the web of logic as the reflected image of the causal sequence of the perceived world, concepts and forms of thought, on their side, having as their deposit, language.

Even the most self-evident judgments are based upon some logical conclusion, even when we are not aware of it. Thus the statement, "The Earth exists", is arrived at by the following syllogism : "What I see exists; I see the Earth : therefore the Earth exists." Thus a statement only needs to be shaped in the form of a syllogism to ascertain whether it is true or not. Everything arrived at by reason, must be perceived in some form or other. In other cases, the activity of the reasoning faculty can only be compared to a loom running empty. Despite its noise, it is producing nothing.

Clearly, a false cognition may be caused, either by there being no perception at all at the base of the reason's activity, or else by the perception of the object cognized being a false one, or penetrating it insufficiently. In the latter case the abstract reproduction by the reason of the phenomenon perceived is bound to be wrong. Finally, a false cognition may be caused by the laws of reason being violated during the process of translating the phenomenon in itself, correctly perceived, into abstract form.

This translation of what is perceived into the higher conceptional form of cognition corresponds to the plastic reproduction of something seen by an artist. This type of reproduction will be the more perfect, the more truly and profoundly the artist perceived the thing in question, and the greater his mastery of the technique of his art. In the Neo-Vedic period, which lasted from about 1,000 to 500 B.C., there arose the great men of the Brahman caste. They regarded themselves as the successors of the Ṛiṣis, and, like all beings, were agitated by the horror of the transitory nature of their own corporeality. Aware that they themselves were the source of that horror, they cultivated *inward contemplation*. Thus they reached the view that their substance, their true 'I' or Self, the Ātman, was behind their corporeality. This being the case, it was not touched by the death of the body, and so were immortal. They tried to discover what awaited them after death by inward contemplation, as by this means they endeavoured to ascertain the possible states of their substantial 'I' or Self beyond the transient body. For this purpose, they isolated themselves, and sought to separate themselves from the external world, including their material body and the life of the senses. Their aim was to achieve pure thinking *without any objective perception*. It was, in fact, to transcend the logic which depends on sense perception.

The result of this was that they saw themselves in this extreme state of detachment wholly untouched in their existence. In fact, their awareness of the positive and actual nature of their Self stood out with ever greater definition the farther they continued the process of detachment. Indeed, this awareness first dawned on them in all its glory at the highest point at which they had left behind them everything knowable, although at this summit their 'I' or Self, apart from their awareness of its actual and positive nature, had become incapable of being grasped or defined. "... invisible, ungraspable, grounded only in the certainty of its own I or Self, beyond the entire extension of the world, full of bliss. This is the fourth quarter, this is the Self, this we should know."

"Knowing outwards" is the first quarter. The state of sleep, "knowing inwards", is the second quarter. The state of deep sleep, "knowing neither outwards nor inwards", is the third quarter.[1]

Thus the Brahmin reached the highest summit of wisdom. Man's highest possible state appeared to be realized, and the final goal attained. The 'I' or Self, freed of all transient and sorrowful attributes, is eternal, complete in itself and full of bliss. The supreme God was discovered in our inner nature, beyond our empirical self, as the real and true Self. But as this 'I' or Self is 'without personality', as Meister Eckhart would say, expressions such as God and deity involving a personal element are not applicable to it. So a special description was applied to the super-personal, truly divine, truly holy fourth quarter. This was simply the Brahman, "the Holy One." The original meaning of Brahman is prayer,[2] and the prayer of the Brahmin was a submersion into their own depths, a devotional submersion. Thus these men described as "the holy," "the Brahman" the most sacred reality they discovered in their prayer.

Imagine a being whose reasoning activities have ceased, and who, therefore, dwells in complete mental and bodily isolation, but is able to apprehend perfectly everything presented to its senses. Such a being, unable to reason, could never arrive at thoughts or concepts. It would remain limited to immediate perception. With this it would be wholly satisfied, since for such a being such perception would constitute perfect apprehension, and it would be in no need whatever of mind and reasoning. Such a being could not be aware of itself, to its 'I'. For the thought or concept of 'I' can only appear in consciousness as the result of the activity of reason, which this imagined being does not possess. Such a being would not think, "I perceive", because it could not think at all, in the sense of reflecting and abstracting. Nevertheless, this being would be conscious of its 'I' after a certain fashion, namely, it would perceive everything as an *object*, as something opposed to itself. Therewith, is the thing perceived it would also lay hold of its own actuality which, so to say, is *reflected*

1. *Māṇḍūkya-Up.*, 7.
2. See George Grimm's *Wissenschaft des Buddhismus* p. 300.

by this thing which thereby becomes an *object.* In the perception of a thing as an object the reality of the *subject* is also indirectly perceived, if the object is really seen as an *object.* For which reason Schopenhauer said : "Of things we have direct knowledge, of ourselves only indirect knowledge."

The perception of every object is bound to give rise to the thought of the subject, even though the subject cannot be perceived. For there can be no perception without a perceiver, and without a perceiver apprehension of a thing would never get itself translated into the abstract form of cognition. Further, if the translation of what is perceived into the higher form of cognition is perfect, then in this higher form of cognition it must also become evident that the subject only presents itself *indirectly* to perception. This *indirect perceptive* apprehending can only be expressed in the rational form of, "This is *not* my I." By the term 'I' one designates oneself as the subject over against the object, thereby giving to the latter the character of object. By qualifying the thing perceived as *not* one's 'I', we acknowledge that the 'I' does not immediately present itself to our perception, but that it is merely the thing perceived which, as the thing perceived, reminds us of the subject which perceives it.

Accordingly, since a being endowed with perfect perception apprehends everything that can be perceived, and supremely so its own personality, as mere *object,* in passing from the perceptive to the reflective activity of reason, our imagined being can arrive at the I-idea only in its negative form. He can only grasp the idea of Not-I thus : "Everything is *not* my I, not my true essence, is *Anattā.*"

This perfect method of cognition (*ñāṇa,* also called *ñāṇadassana*), which is meditative contemplation combined with a cognition perfectly in accord with "reality as it is", is what the Buddha teaches. Because the 'I' or Self is not perceivable, and is 'not to be found' in any way, the Buddha never occupied himself with it. He even describes all statements relating to this Self as empty fancies. He concerns himself only with the things of the world which he summarizes in the elements of personality (*sakkāva*). Those things which are cognizable he saw correctly as mere objects and so not our true Self (*Anattā*). To the I-idea in its positive form :

"This am I", one comes when, contrary to *fact*, one confounds oneself with the knowable; that is, with one's ego.

It will now be seen how right the Buddha was to admonish against the search for the Self. For there remained for the true Self nothing of the world and so no possibility of understanding it in any way. The word Self is the greatest of all *equivoques*. Each man has his own definition of it, and it rarely accords with that of anyone else.

Thus, step by step, we have come to a subversion of all concepts. Hitherto, we regarded ourselves as belonging to the world and as consisting of its own elements. Nothing, being the contrary of Everything, meant for us the total annihilation of the universe and of ourselves. The Buddha showed most clearly that the world is essentially foreign to our deepest Self. We see ourselves inexplicably involved in it, so that it is to us in all its details an inscrutable riddle. Only one thing we cannot doubt, the suffering it causes us:

"Mysterious is everything,
Only one thing not, and that is our pain."

This inverted manner in which the saint looks at the world, as compared with that of the average man, is hinted at by the Buddha himself, when he says: "What in the world is regarded as true, that by the saints is regarded as false, as it really is, rightly, in accordance with perfect wisdom. What in the world is regarded as false, that by the saints is regarded as true, as it really is, rightly, in accordance with perfect wisdom."[1]

The Buddha, in teaching men to consider their situation with careful thought, restored to man his capacity for wonder in fullest measure, so that he again feels himself to be a stranger in the world, in his own body and even in what he calls his personality. He also revealed to his disciples that they no longer share the fate of the other inhabitants of the island, who neither know who they are nor where they came from. The Buddha's disciples know at last that the ocean of Nothingness contains "the island, the unique." In this Nothing has been recognized the real essence, the eternal home. *Attham gata*, he who went home, is the description given to the deceased saint.

The Nothing that was so long regarded as the mesaureless black pail spread over the abyss of annihilation into

1. *Sutta-Nipāta* III, 12.

which every living being must eventually fall, is now seen as the mysterious veil overlying man's mysterious essence. It is only necessary to pass behind it to escape suffering forever. When we disappear from the world, becoming nothing cognizable, nothing for the world itself, but not nothing for ourselves. On leaving the world there is left behind the only thing still belonging to it—our corpse. Everything else we long before relinquished, and thus we proceed to the glory of our Self. "Liberated of what we call body, sensation, perception, mentations, consciousness, the Perfected One is deep, immeasurable, unfathomable, like the great ocean."

The detachment from material corporeality to the highest spiritual goal naturally occurs stage by stage. And it is by what might be called "spiritual exercises" that this spirituality is attained. "Ask not what is divine; for if you are not so, you know it not even if you hear it."[1] And again : "If paradise is not first within you, then assuredly believe me that you will never enter it."[2] And Hölderlin said, "Only those who believe in the divine are it themselves."[3] "Let man be noble, oh ritable and good. For this alone distinguishes him from all the beings we know. Hail to the *unknown higher beings whom we divine* ! Let man be like them, and may his example teach us to believe in them."[4]

This throws the first correct light on the doctrine of Reincarnation in the cycle of rebirths to which the Aryan Indian has adhered with self-assured conviction from time immemorial. If man's essence is not touched by death, then for the person who does not already in his present existence find his way back into the Holy, the Brahman, there is left no other possibility except rebirth to a new existence which is more suitable to him, and in which he can continue to strive towards his home.

The core of the doctrine of Reincarnation is expounded with perfect clarity in the *Bṛhadāraṇyaka-Upaniṣad* 4, 4, 2-6, where it says : "Then (after the soul has departed from its previous body) the self has particular consciousness, and goes to the

1. Angelus Silesius.
2. Ibid.
3. Friedrich Holderlin.
4. Johann Wolfgang Goethe.

body which is related to that consciousness .... Just as a goldsmith takes apart a little quantity of gold and fashions another—a newer and better—form, so does the self throw this body away, or make it senseless, and make another —a newer and better form .... As it does and acts, so it becomes; by doing good it becomes good, and by doing evil it becomes evil .... it becomes virtuous through good acts and vicious through evil acts. Others, however, say, 'The self is identified with desire alone. What it desires, it resolves; what is resolves, it works out; and what it works out, it attains.' "

From this view of man the later Aryan Indian derived the following moral principles that were obligatory to all his fellow-countrymen : 1) charity, 2) uprightness, 3) not to injure any living being, 4) truthfulness, 5) selfcontrol. He even beat out the roll of the thunder as *Damyata* ! *Datta*! *Dayatvam* !—"Restrain yourselves! Give alms! Have compassion !"[1]

This morality was so universally observed that many an Indian prince could claim : "In my kingdom there is no thief, no miser, no drunkard, no one who would not make sacrifices, no one not versed in the Veda, no rake, no harlot." Such morality is brought to maturity by the belief in rebirth, if it is associated with the conviction that the nature of the future existence is determined by actions in the present.

Those who wished to escape from the cycle of rebirths and hence from the world, had to practice self-castigation and renunciation (*nyāsa*). Self-castigation meant gradually mortifying instinct and impulse and so acquiring all the virtues. It consisted in the voluntary acceptance of privations, such as undertaking penance and fasting, in order to weaken to the utmost the craving for earthly pleasures. Renunciation was the radical means. This entailed detachment from wife and family and from all external possessions. The ascetics traversed the country as wandering mendicants or lived as forest hermits. The highest renunciation was practised by the *sannyāsin*. He wandered through the land in rags or wearing only a loin-cloth. His food was exceedingly frugal, and at the highest stage the clay vessel for receiving it was "his belly or his hand". He spent the maximum time in silence and meditation which caused him to regard his body as carrion. His goal was the Brahman.

1. Cp. T.S. Eliot's use of it in his *The Waste Land*.

Thus the great question as to whether, having regard to our relation to suffering, it is possible to escape from it, is solved. It is possible. Suffering is rooted in the structure of the world, in being as a whole, as well as in all its component parts, all being subject to the law of transitoriness. This is the world we experience with our six senses, in our personality and *as* our personality. But personality is something alien to our true essence. From this alien presence we need only to free ourselves to become free of the world of suffering, and from the suffering of the world—that is, from suffering altogether. The possibility of this liberation the Buddha expressly asserts in the following words : "There really is liberation from corporeality, from sensation, from perception, from mentation, from consciousness, therefore creatures do liberate themselves from corporeality, from sensation, from perception, from mentation, from consciousness."

This insights however fundamental, is not sufficient. For it gives rise to that greatest of all questions : *How* can this liberation be realized ? How can we vanquish the ego and the whole world and reach our own proper realm ? The realm "where there is neither birth nor sickness nor becoming old nor dying, nor woe, sorrow, suffering, grief and despair." How can we, *by visible evidence*, prove ourselves to be beyond the world and all its suffering ? If the Buddha did answer this question, then he did indeed bestow on all mankind the greatest imaginable benefit.

The Buddha is wholly awakened from the dream of life. This is both the sense and the literal meaning of the word Buddha. But to what has Buddha awakened ? He has awakened to the supreme reality, to that reality which Schopenhauer divined when he said : "When we wake up from a dream that vividly affects us, it is not so much its disappearance as the discovery of a second reality which lay concealed under that (of the dream) so deeply stirring us, and which now emerges. We really all have a lasting divination or presentiment also under this reality in which we live and are there lies hidden a second and different reality. It is the thing-in-itself, the (reality proper) to this (the present life's dream)."

A Buddha, however, has not merely wakened to the supreme reality. He also presents his highest knowledge, which is superior to that of "all gods and men," and he presents it directly and clearly, free of all mythological disguise and mythical clothing. It is given in so cogent a form that it presents itself as self-evident to the person able to follow him. For this reason a Buddha does not demand belief; he provides knowledge. "Well are you invested with this Marvel (this doctrine of the Buddha), with this clearly visible thing that is at all times accessible and says : 'Come and see!' Men of judgment and discretion can find it in their own interior."

We imagine that truth is equivalent to immediate intuitive perception, whereas perception is simply the source of truth. Intuition, or immediate perception, is a perception of the five external senses, a sensuous perception, or an intuitively direct perception by means of the sixth sense, the sense of intuitive thought. This latter perception is limited to the intuitive perception of space, of knowledge itself as such, and of the state that is devoid of object. This immediate perception (sensuous or intellectual or intuitively immediate) is wholly without words or concepts. For this reason, it cannot be communicated by words, but only by transferring it to another kind of perception, perhaps by way of artistic work.

Abstract knowledge receives the whole of its content from direct, sense-perceived knowledge. It borrows its materials entirely from the latter. Therefore it is unable to give any new knowledge. It simply serves to condense our direct knowledge, once gained, into settled concepts, and thus to fix that knowledge and transmit it to others. Accordingly truth, that is the adequate apprehension of something existing in the intellect of man, may ultimatety be gained only through one's own immediate perception.

Only direct, sense-perceived knowledge gives complete satisfaction. Whoever possesses this has no further need of faith. He who possesses it no longer concerns himself with merely abstract knowledge, with all its possibilities of error. He who has become certain of a thing because he himself has perceived it, no more needs to believe in its existence than he needs to have its existence proved to him.

It is only the highest degree of truth which can wholly and permanently satisfy man with regard to the primal problem as to whether it is possible to overcome suffering and, above all, death. And our age demands this highest degree of truth. Just as in the field of science, no man is satisfied with speculation, possibilities or mere hope, so in the crucial realms of suffering and death, no man can be satisfied with exhortations to believe. *Our age demands proof, and it will be satisfied with nothing less.* The demand is to *see* in order to *know* which was precisely the approach made by the Buddha. He did not demand faith; he provided knowledge. What is more, he showed men how they can see for themselves and so know for themselves. The teaching of the Buddha is a triumph of logic. Whereas in so many other religions there must be a large measure of credulity, and even, in some instance, faith in defiance of observed fact; in the teaching of the Buddha there is no venturing beyond the knowledge, nor is there any going beyond the knowledge every man can, by observation, acquire for himself. In all the realms of knowledge, no discovery equals this in importance and in worth.

This was the triumph of the Buddha, who, some two and a half millennia ago, succeeded in crystallizing out this great, primary problem of mankind. He freed it from all accessories of every kind, and abstracted from it all obscure by-products so frequently introduced into the problem by the longing for metaphysical knowledge. He claimed to have solved the problem in such a way that every one by his own direct perception, by his own immediate insight, might discover for himself the correctness of the solution, and could prove it by testing it upon himself. This is the teaching of Gotama the Buddha, the Awakened One, the culminating point in Indian Wisdom.

The solution of the problem of suffering was the task he set himself when he realised the burden of human anguish. For this purpose he renounced his claim to his father's throne, he rejected riches and separated himself from his wife and son whom he loved dearly. He exchanged all the advantages and luxuries of the world for the life of a homeless mendicant. When he was born, the Brahmins living as priests and astrologers at his father's court when the Buddha, then Prince Siddhārtha, was a child predicted : "If Prince Siddhārtha mounts the throne, he will become a king of kings, a ruler of the world; but if he renounces the throne and chooses the life of an ascetic, then he will become an overcomer of the world, a perfect Buddha." While the ascetic, Asita, prophesied: "This child will one day become a most perfect Buddha and show men the way to liberation."

The sight of sickness, old age and death caused him to leave his palace with all that it meant to him and he spent seven years enduring the self-mortification which Indians believe leads soonest to the perception of truth. This served to convince him of the uselessness of all painful asceticism. He then immersed himself in queste of inward contemplation, and which, at last, brought him the solution to his great problem.

The Buddha obtained his truths by way of logical inference, and he teaches them in this same form. In the 12th. dialogue of the *Majjhima-Nikāya* he lays special emphasis on the logical character of his teaching. The teaching of the Buddha is, in fact, a *religion of reason.* In the Canon it is characterized directly by the epithet *vibhajjavāda*, which means religion of logic or reason.

There is a serious danger of error when the concept or judgment cannot be traced back directly to the underlying intuitive knowledge and thus to reality, but only be means of several, or a long chain of syllogisms. This is in contrast to those concepts and judgments which in their premises have their *immediate* ground in intuitive perception. And it is this danger we have in mind when we speak of the inferior value of *merely demonstrated* truths.

Action based on nothing more than intuition is equivalent to impulsive conduct. Far superior is conduct that is guided by reflection, by a deliberation that tests and compares. When our times again undertake their "transvaluation of all values"[1] by attaching more weight to intuition than to reflection, they are simply displaying a further sign of decadence. Evolution resulted in the extreme of admitting only the reasoning faculty's activity and the almost total exclusion of intuition. The reaction to this was the claim that "pure intuition" is the exclusive source of knowledge, and that

1. Friedrich Wilhelm Nietzsche, *Thus Spake Zarathustra, Beyond Good and Evil* and *The Will to Power.*

reason (rationalism) can discover nothing of reality. In this way, our age moves in extremes and in extremes which lead to decadence. Reflection is the second potential of knowledge, and its exercise calls for effort and exertion, which is regarded as sufficient reason for discarding it as not modern.

As everywhere, so here truth lies in the centre. Intuition and Reflection belong inseparably to each other, since only reflection, based only on intuitive perception and never venturing beyond this, brings us knowledge and, consequently, truth.

"The deathless has been attained. I will instruct you, I will impart to you the doctrine. Following my instructions, ye shall know and realize that utmost noble goal of the holy life for yourselves even in this present lifetime." And, in fact, the disciples the Buddha addressed soon attained to the "incomparable security, the birthless, the free from growth and decay and disease, the deathless, the sorrowless, the stainless." They attained the end of suffering.

The gospel of the termination of suffering from then on constituted the only theme of the Buddha, the Awakened One, as he thereafter called himself.

He devoted the following forty-five years to its propagation. Every day—nay, every hour he could say of himself: "As before so also now, I preach only suffering and the Cessation of Suffering." He said: "As the great ocean is penetrated by only one taste, the taste of salt, even so this Doctrine and this order are penetrated by only one taste, the taste of salvation."[1] This, *the sole content of his teaching*, he made externally knowable by condensing it into the Four Most Excellent Truths of Suffering, within which everything good is contained:" . . . all things whatsoever that are good and salutary are contained and comprehended in the Four Most Excellent Truths, namely in these: The Most Excellent Truth of Suffering, the Most Excellent Truth of the Arising of Suffering, the Most Excellent Truth of the Ceasing of Suffering and the Most Excellent Truth of the Path that leads to the Ceasing of Suffering."[2]

1. *Majj. Nik*., 22. Discourse.
2. Ibid.

The Buddha's knowledge was by no means restricted to these four truths. His mind penetrated the enigmas of existence in other directions, and more deeply than any other mortal. But he deliberately withheld this knowledge from mankind.

". . . What I have perceived and have not communicated to you is much more than what I have communicated to you. And why have I not revealed this to you? Because it would not be of advantage to you, because it does not promote the higher life in all its purity, because it does not lead to disgust with the world, to annihilation of all lust, to the ceasing of the transitory, to peace, to higher knowledge, to awakening, to *Nibbāṇa*. Therefore I have not communicated it to you. And what have I communicated to you? What suffering is; what the Arising of Suffering is; what the Ceasing of Suffering is, and what the Path that leads to the Ceasing of Sufiering I have communicated to you."[1]

The Buddha even goes so far as to reject the setting up of problems that go beyond this exclusively practical purpose. All theoretical questions and all speculative enquiries, particularly about the essence of the world and of ourselves, he dismisses as leading only into "a blind alley of views", and thus involving the inexperienced mortal in deeper suffering.

Accordingly, the Buddha teaches no system of philosophy, no kind of metaphysics, no ontology nor demonology. He is not concerned about the origin of the world, its duration and its laws, since any such enquiry must be without any practical purpose for mankind. These matters have interest for him only insofar as they are of practical value for the annihilation of suffering. The enigma of the world belongs to those enigmas "with which to dabble only leads to perplexity". Those who address themselves to such problems he likens to explorers who find themselves in a desert where they are beset by wild beasts. Instead of addressing themselves to the task of defending themselves against these animals, they embark upon zoological studies of them, and so end up being devoured by the beasts, together with the fruits of their studies. He then pointed out the lesson in greater detail: ". . . anyone who

1. *Sam. Nik.*, XXII, 94.

should say, 'I will not lead the religious life under the Blessed One until the Blessed One shall elucidate to me either that the world is eternal, or that the world is not eternal . . . or that the saint exists or does not exist after death,' that person would die before the Accomplished one had ever elucidated this to him.

The religious life does not depend on the dogma that the world is eternal, nor does it depend on the dogma that the world is not eternal. Whether the dogma obtains that the world is eternal, or that the world is not eternal, there still remain birth, old age, death, sorrow, lamentation, misery, grief and despair, for the extinction of which in the present life I am prescribing."[1]

This is another sign of the surpassing wisdom of the Buddha. He communicated only sufficient to save mankind from desperation. Anything more would only distract the mind from the great goal of concentrating all our forces upon this salvation. This does not mean that the Buddha teaches that the Four Excellent Truths exhaust all truths. He admits all verities the human mind has found and may yet find. He accepts them because they are true, and some he incorporates into his teaching. One of these is the doctrine of reincarnation. "That . . . which the wise declare does not exist in the world, that I also declare not to exist; and what the wise declare to exist in the world, that I also declare to exist."[2] But he does not admit these verities as distinguishing points in his doctrine.

The Buddha brings immediately before our consciousness the principal and cardinal problem of our life . . .how to escape suffering and, above all, the suffering of death. He does more. He promises us its solution in the highest possible form of certitude, that is, by the awakening of our own direct cognition. His doctrine is, first, free from every wrapping of a mythological or allegorical character, such as is peculiar to religions. The Buddha also rejects every kind of theorising: He says of himself, "The Accomplished One is free from every

1. *Majj. Nik.*, 39. Discourse.
2. *Sam. Nik.*, XXII, 94.

theory, for he has *seen*."[1] Not even with logical conclusions, in one way or another for sake of immediate perception does the Buddha concern himself. The sole criterion of truth for him is, and always remains, intuitive apprehension of truth. It is on the self-evident consequence of this standpoint that he does not claim any belief in his own purely descriptive exposition of the things he says he knows by his direct perception. He even admonishes his disciples to accept nothing, not even from himself, simply on good faith. They are to accept only fact as they themselves have seen it.

". . . What you say is only what you yourselves have recognised, what you yourselves have comprehended, what you yourselves have understood. Given are ye to this teaching, the clearly visible, the timeless, the all-inviting, which is to be understood by every reasonable man."[2]

Again: "Do not believe in hearsay, nor in traditions, nor in rumours, nor in the word handed down, nor in purely logical conclusions, nor in external semblance, nor because of agreement of anything with the views you cherish and approve of, nor because of your own thinking of anything that is true. Neither shall you think: 'The ascetic, the Buddha himself, is my teacher, but if you, yourself, gain the insight: Such things are evil, such things lead to misfortune and suffering, then you may reject them."[3]

The Buddha's whole method of consideration goes back to this. From the first, it stipulates a *meditative* thinking which becomes contemplation. Meditation, thoughtfulness, contemplation and deliberation are the means of discovering truth. In the doctrine of the Buddha meditation becomes the means of the profoundest knowledge.

It produces a discerning contemplation. In the beginning there is a faint *presentiment* of the truth. This becomes a *belief in the truth* interspersed with doubts, and finally a complete *logical comprehension*, culminating in a *palpably intuitive penetration of* its object. This penetration forever dispels all doubt. The truth is then *experienced* by us by our *thoroughly*

1. *Majj. Nik.*, 72 Discourse.
2. *Ibid.* 38 Discourse.
3. *Aṅg. Nik.*, IV, 193.

penetrating its object with the spiritual eye. In this way, with such clarity, a man must *experience* all the elements of his personality as not the I or Self as essentially foreign to himself. This he must do to experience immediately in his own body the absolute bliss of complete *desirelessness* which ensues as a result of this 'vision'.

The premises of the Buddha's judgments and conclusions are found at any moment and without trouble in intuitive perceptive reality, a characteristic that represents the formal part of the cognitive activity of *all* men of genius. A classical proof of this is given in the fact that the Buddha's statements are interspersed with parables drawn from reality. These occur in full measure and, at times, in a striking manner. Parables are pre-eminently suitable for verifying abstract ideas as the reflected image of intuitive reality. For this reason every inspired mind feels the need to give clarity to his abstract ideas through similes and parables. The Buddha was greatly impressed with the discernment that abstract knowledge is of value which can always and easily be shown to be based on intuitive reality. He was so penetrated with this idea that he enjoined on those who entered his Order to make clear to themselves and to others, by parables and thus by going back to the reality of intuitive perception, the knowledge his teaching had to convey to them. A judgment or proposition which cannot be illustrated by a simile from reality has, in fact, no real value.

The Buddha's teaching is based on intuitive *thinking*, which for this reason he demands. He also expressly states this character of his teaching in the standing sentence : "This doctrine is profound, hard to see, difficult to perceive, calm, sublime, *not in the sphere of merely abstract* thought, subtle, to be grasped only by sages." He had good reason to stress that his teaching is not accessible to merely abstract thought, as, in his day, dialectic, the art of disputation, flourished in India. Using merely abstract concepts, and in the guise of logic, it was infallibly demonstrated that "everything is" and also that "nothing is" ; that "all is unity" and that "all is plurality". The false element did not consist in the fact that men worked with the laws of logic, but in their tossing about ready-made concepts (*takka*) according to the laws of logic.

Logic originally meant to reckon ; to take into account, consider and reason. According to this, *logical thinking* means thinking in conformity with the laws of reason. It indicates that procedure of the faculty of reason, of the logos, which that faculty observes when left to itself, and hence in the solitary thinking of a rational being who is not led astray by anything, whether by material or abstract representations, or with representations of *intuitive perception*. In the light of this method of the Master, and guided by his own words, there is revealed to us in the teaching of the Buddha an understanding of the cycle of rebirths in all its height and depth.

This entails following a path—the Path of Enlightenment—on which the Buddha's teaching becomes easy to understand to every man of intelligence and good will, at least to the extent of teaching him to comprehend the cycle of his rebirths with the possibility of *controlling* it. With this he experiences in his meditations the firm foundation of all genuine religiosity, and in this the inner peace and *genuine* gladness of which our age no longer possesses even a trace.

The teaching is a gradual unfolding of truth. Only our own immediate insight is of value, and the Buddha's doctrine itself has value only insofar as it makes this our own insight possible.

"The Teacher expounds the Teaching more and more deeply, more and more highly, in all its divisions wholesome and unwholesome. According as the Teacher proceeds to expound the teaching to the disciple, the disciple arrives at certitude as respects point after point in the Teaching. For such reasons, upon such grounds, through such tokens, faith is fixed on the Accomplished One, has struck root, is settled fast, such is called *reasonable* faith, faith *grounded in sight*, firm, not to be shaken by any ascetic or recluse or god or devil or by anyone in all the world." "Not directly at the beginning may certainty be gained, but gradually striving, gradually struggling, striding on pace by pace, certainty is attained .... A man full of trust comes near .... he works, and because he works earnestly, *with his own person he realizes* the supreme truth and, wisely penetrating, beholds it face to face."[1]

1. *Majj. Nik.*, 70 Discourse.

The Buddha asks only one thing from his disciples : That they should tread the way he himself has shown, upon which one may win the intuitive apprehension of truth. This minimum of trust to try at least once the way shown by him to the discovery of truth, even he cannot omit. But the minimum of trust, entirely indispensible, once given to him and described by the Buddha with the accuracy of an ordnance map, once entered upon, is like the water which primes a pump. Form it all the rest follows. Soon the foretold glimpses of light will appear. Eventually, the faith first given will change into unshakeable certainty as to the correctness of that part of the way yet to be completed.

"To the trusting follower, to the follower training himself in the Master's Order with earnest zeal, the confidence dawns .... To the trusting disciple, to the disciple who trains himself in the Master's Order with earnest zeal, the Master's Order imparts itself, refreshing and precious; in him the confidence dawns : Let skin and tendons and bones shrivel up within my body, let flesh and blood dry up : whatever may be accomplished by human Virtue, human strength and human valour, not till it is accomplished shall my strength lessen." The Buddha asks for no more faith than is given to a guide, but he does not ask less than the faith a guide must claim. "This, O Brahmin I can do in regard to this : A guide is the Accomplished One."[1]

According to the standpoint of the Buddha, all purely abstract notions are wanting in his Discourses. Only those occur which may be drawn from perception and are evident in themselves.

As the Buddha wishes to bring about the individual's own direct perception of truth, the question arises as to what may be the nature of this perception which leads to the extraordinary results he promises ? Its peculiarity cannot lie in the object, since the Buddha has to do only with the world about us. It can, therefore, be nothing other than a peculiar way of looking at things. And indeed its secret consists in a unique deepening of the normal manner of seeing things. The goal the Buddha sets before everyone is this mode of viewing things in the form of pure contemplation. He gives in detail the several steps

1. *Majj. Nik.*, 10 Discourse.

leading upwards to it, and he also teaches the ever greater perfecting of this pure contemplation itself, right up to the culminating point where "it draws aside the veil of the world."

The cognizing part of consciousness becomes entirely separated from the willing part. It is conditioned by such a deep silence of will, on the one hand, and such an energy of the perceptive function, on the other, that even individuality vanishes from consciousness and man is isolated as the pure subject of cognition. By eliminating all and every motion of will, such a complete tranquillity of the mind — *samatha* — must be produced that "thoughts about me and mine no more arise".

The Buddha teaches that the man who works for his own salvation *as well as* for that of others, "is the great, the best, most venerable and the most sublime."[1] He emphasizes that only the man "who is himself not drawn into the swamp can pull out another who is submerged."[2]

This attention to individual and to the salvation of others, has resulted in the teaching of the Buddha leaving its mark on the whole of non-Islamic Asia, and thus on more than half the human race. All Asiatic religions are indebted to it for the noblest moral element that is effective even today. This culminates in kindness to every breathing being — the doctrine of the perfectly Awakened One.

The Buddha, renouncing every explanation of all other phenomena, sought only to find the end of suffering. And, at last, behind the ocean of will, he found another realm, the realm of freedom from suffering, the narrow entrance to this realm disclosing itself to him.

His concentration of all his forces on how to escape suffering led him at last to his goal. Naturally, he made this point the foundation of his unique way of salvation. This may be characterized as a direct and ever deepening envisagement, an ever purer contemplation of suffering, regarded in its causes and in its relation to ourselves. This contemplation constitutes the goal of all insight and the source of all wisdom. Ultimately, all virtue serves only this goal. It does so by creating a pure heart in which the storms of willing have been laid to rest,

1. *Aṅg. Nik.*, IV, 95.
2. *Majj. Nik.*, 8th Discourse.

which is the indispensible antecedent to it. Only he who by the practice of ceaseless mindfulness trains his consciousness little by little to dwell exclusively on the contemplation of suffering, only *he*, "wisely penetrating", will struggle through to that point where arises, ever more distinct, "the island, the only one", where there is no more suffering and no more death. Such a one alone is competent to pass an authoritative judgment upon the truth or untruth of the Buddha's teaching.

The man who denies the truth revealed by the Buddha is likened to a man born blind who denies the existence of the moon and stars because he cannot see them. The one who merely makes an intellectual examination of the teaching cannot see its truth. "That he should perceive the utmost reality, the highest truth, is impossible."[1] It is by contemplation that truth is discerned. Thus there is no element of the vicarious in the teaching of the Buddha. In the *Saṁyutta-Nikāya* it is said that to seek to win peace through others, as by way of priests or sacrificers, is impossible.[2] But those who seek salvation by way of contemplation have always been few. Most men find they prefer to ignore suffering and they shrink from occupying themselves minutely with it. For them there is no help.

The doctrine of the Buddha has as its instrument that most exact of all methods, that of natural science. It requires true men, "no hypocrites, nor dissemblers, unassuming, resolute, stout-hearted, possessing insight, clear-headed, steadfast and of unified mind, wise and intelligent", who alone are capable of applying the experimental method. With them, "the noble ones", he has communication, as with the true aristocrats of mankind, "to whom the world is too mean", and who, therefore, wish to grow out of it. To them he offers that most precious prize, the solution of the world's suffering, which, being based upon one's own immediate perception, provides unshakeable certainty.

This system, wholly scientific is said to be no longer suited to our times ! *For such a contention we must seek the reasons*. And we find, when such statements are not based on pure unreason, that it does not satisfy the modern critics of the Buddha's

1. *Majj. Nik.*, 99 Discourse.
2. *Saṁ. Nik.*, XLII, 6.

doctrine. This type of critic he described as men "who only learn the doctrine so as to be able to give discourses and express opinions about it", instead of practically testing its truth. According to the Buddha, salvation from suffering is identical with salvation from the world itself, and the disciple should try this method of salvation in earnest. This is said to be no longer up-to-date. Now it may be admitted that in our time mankind, either because of his high civilization or on account of it, is devoted in an unprecedented degree to a materialistic conception of the world, even where, theoretically, this is held in abhorrence. Precisely on this account, all consciousness of the unsuitability of their continued stay in this world, and so of the necessity of salvation, is wanting in men.

But there remain a choice few who feel far from satisfied with this world, and therefore wish to grow out of it. For these the gospel of salvation through one's own strength, and in such wise that its occurrence is *directly perceived and experienced within oneself*, is the most tremendous of all events. For such the doctrine of the Buddha is modern, quite as modern as any branch of natural science whose methods it shares. To those few, the doctrine of the Buddha, who himself called it "the timeless", will be modern for all time, in the same way that a definitive solution of a problem remains valid for all time.

In an age when the world is "too much with us", it may be hard to accept the truth that whoever desires to obtain *entire* deliverance from the world, in this life must wholly forsake it ; must leave it completely behind him. But the Buddha recognized that there are those who realize that their destiny lies beyond this world, but who prefer to make their way towards this goal within the world. He points out to these that they need not return to this world after death. Instead, they may realise the great goal in one of the highest worlds of light. Because he knows the path leading out of this world, he also knows the paths within which lead to a fortunate rebirth and he shows these with indisputable certainty. His doctrine is modern in this sense also, that it assures to each man of the world who is concerned about his future after death, the measure of freedom from suffering and of well-being procurable for him.

"If this doctrine should be attainable only for monks and

nuns, but not for his male and female adherents, *living the household life, abstaining in chastity, and satisfying their desires,* then this holy life would be incomplete just because of this."[1] *Nibbāṇa* shows itself to be *eternal rest,* "eternal stillness", the "GREAT PEACE" whose realm the delivered one enters even during this lifetime, which he realizes completely at death, and in which he has taken possession for ever of everything "true and real". This GREAT PEACE is far superior to all "perfect well-being" and "blissful rest" that can be won here below. Such is insufficient, as it has the defect of being produced, and "what is in any way produced is changeable and must perish." It does not lead beyond transitoriness and suffering. *Eternal*—unchanging—rest is alone the state free from suffering. For where no change occurs, nothing more, not even the redeemed one himself, can arise through grasping : "But, monk, a sage who is at peace is not born, does not age, is not agitated, does nor envy. As there is nothing by which he can be born, how could he die ? Not dying, how could he be agitated ? Not being agitated, how could he envy ? When it is said 'Where there is stability, conceit and boasting do not continue in existence, and when they do not continue in existence the sage is said to be at peace,' it is said in reference to this."[2] He does not incline, and so he neither comes or goes, appears nor disappears, and so "there is no here nor there nor between; this is the end of suffering," yea, it is pure blessedness. "Bliss is *Nibbāṇa* !" It is the highest bliss. For rest, peace and blessedness are fundamentally the same : Whoso is impregnated with goodness .... who cleaves to the doctrine of the Buddha, turns towards the *peaceful state,* where transitoriness finds rest."

Death belongs to life just as much as birth. It is nothing but the actual *moment* of our great life in all the worlds, in which the corporeal organism used is relinquished, and grasping of a new germ of life takes place. The opposite of life is rest, since life is movement. But this rest is only definitively reached by holiness, from which the self-deception involved in such expressions as "rest of the grave", "rest of the dead", becomes at once evident.

1. *Majj. Nik.*, 73 Discourse.
2. *Ibid.*, 140 Discourse, translated by J.B. Horner.

Here, once more, "normal" understanding will be inclined to protest. How can bliss exist where there is such absolute rest that nothing more of any sort can be felt? when Sāriputta exclaimed, "Bliss is *Nibbāṇa*, bliss is *Nibbāṇa*!" he was asked, "How can there be bliss where there is no sensation?" Like the questioner, the modern sceptic may not understand Sāriputta's reply: "This precisely, O friend, is bliss, that here there is no sensation."

CHAPTER-3

CONCLUSION

The Application of Metaphysical Wisdom To Practical Life

> "We may consider religion as a set of symbols that may be institutionalized, considered as normative, in a society or internalized in a personality."[1]

Perfect happiness resides in the Absolute. This is the translation of the final result of the Buddha's doctrine into the terminology of Western philosophy. In the latter, the concept of the absolute is confusingly obscure and is riddled with contradictions. But the Buddha uses the concept of the absolute in its literal and original sense, in which it is instantly clear.

The Latin word *absolutus* is the past participle of *absolvere*, which means 'to loosen, to detach'. Therefore 'absolute' literally means detached, and the Absolute is 'the loosened', the detached'. In Pāli, the language of the Buddhist Canon, the word *vimutta* is the word used by the Buddha when he speaks of one who has become holy, a 'Perfect One.' And in Pāli, the language of the Buddhist Canon, the word has exactly the same meaning .... 'to release, to detach.' *Vimutta* is identical with Absolute.

The Buddha proclaimed as the ultimate goal of the holy course of life deliverance or release, the attaining of the absolute. He speaks only of the absolute Self, which he calls a 'Perfect One', and so uses the concept of the Absolute in the sense in which it can be realized, and in which for that very reason it is real. To this Absolute the concept of being no

1. Robert N. Bellah, *Religion and Progress in Modern Asia*, New York 1965, p. 171.

longer applies.[1] Nor is the Absolute of the Buddha either reason or knowledge, as is the absolute of Western philosophers. He calls the substratum of the phenomenal world, and thus what is termed the absolute reality, the 'realm of *Nibbāṇa*', free from all attributes.

The absolute of the Buddha is not any knowledge, for the saint who has become absolute has also detached himself from all consciousness. This is the greatest obstacle to men to become reconciled to this idea of the absolute or to aspire to it. This, too, is the result of ignorance. As we know, all consciousness is directed outwards on to the five groups of personality. Only about this can we know anything at all. But a consciousness of such a nature is the most terrible thing there can be. For, on account of such a nature, this consciousness conveys to us only a knowledge of sorrowful and painful things. For the man who has grasped this, consciousness is no longer a good thing. But this is not the consciousness meant by the average man who has made himself acquainted with the Buddha's doctrine, when he is afraid of a state lacking in consciousness. What he is thinking he cannot do without this consciousness of absolute contentedness and boundless peace, when once he has become perfect. But even this consciousness is merely awareness of the elements of personality—the consciousness which has become free from these elements and so is perfectly happy. It is the consciousness of *anattā* in contrast to the delusion that the personality is our Self. Therefore even this consciousness of *anattā* is possible only as long as we are burdened with the elements of personality. This is all the more so since this consciousness is possible only with the help of a bodily organism as the apparatus for producing all consciousness. As long as we are burdened with a body, we are not released from the suffering of transitoriness. Thus he who seeks eternal freedom from suffering and thus for eternal happiness, must forego consciousness of this eternal happiness.

Further, the man who has secured the eternal happiness of the perfect state would find eternal consciousness of this state intolerable. This is obvious. As soon as the saint has fully realized the vision of anattā, and as soon as he sees with per-

1. Grimm, *Doctrine of the Buddha*, p. 133.

fect clarity that his body and his consciousness ceaselessly arise and pass away, while he, himself, remains untouched by all this, he has the supreme knowledge that this body and consciousness are no part of his essential Self, but are mere attributes of the Self. For supreme knowledge consists in immediate perception. He also perceives that all suffering is only the suffering of the constant transitoriness of his body and his consciousness. This produces a disgust with his body and his consciousness, a reaction which causes him to detach himself. When this happens, he experiences the inexpressible wellbeing of detachment—he has become absolute. Consciousness of this wellbeing is the only consciousness in which he takes delight. He experiences the bliss of deliverance.

Even this consciousness of one who has become absolute becomes superfluous. For one who has become perfect, it would be an unbearabable affliction were he to be conscious for ever of the fact of his freedom from all personality. This would be an intolerable disturbance of his Great Peace. "Free from disturbance are the saints."

The "Great Theorem or Syllogism" represents the most perfect reflection and sets forth the results of this reflection in a logical train of thought. In the words and sentences used by the Buddha, inevitably there remains "only a lingering trace." But it is one which a perfectly Awakened One could sketch with the greatest possible clearness. Only a man with a religious turn of mind, who is also a "passive genius," to use Jean Paul's phrase, is able to grasp such an idea. Thus, shortly after the Buddha's death, the *anattā*-idea was no longer understood. And, indeed, it has been turned into its very opposite.

Soon, the Buddha's followers and interpreters were saying there was no 'I', no Self at all. That he was concerned with the Not-Self has caused too many to imagine that he presupposed there was no Self. In fact, he repeated again and again, "This belongs not to me, this am I not, this is not *my* Self, precisely because he affirmed the reality of the 'I', the Self. The denial of the Self never entered his thoughts. To deny the Self is to declare oneself to be nothing, "at which all thinking turns away", as the Upaniṣads say. For a nothing could neither deny nor explain anything. To deny this reality of the Self is to flee in the face of all experience.

A man cannot debate on his Self as a fact, but simply in what the Self consists, or in what it does not consist. For the Buddha, indeed, this was the point in question. With the meditation exercises it is not a case of recognizing the factors of personality as not a self, but as seeing through these factors as not being *one's own Self*, which is a radically different matter, and one which the Buddha was the first to perceive. The great sin is egoism which, in the arrogant statement "this am I" limits all care and attention to one's own personality. Therefore the Buddha describes as the very opposite of the *anattā*-idea that "I-am-arrogance", in consequence of which we identify ourselves with our personality.

To have reached full development means to have attained supreme cognition; but this is obtained when all materiality is seen as being inadequate to us. For this reason, the man who is released gives up his material "attributes" and achieves a state of absolute immateriality. In it 'he returns to his origin'. Said Goethe, "What belongs to you not, you must eschew— What disturbs your mind, you shouldn't endure." The Buddhist saint, aware of this, divests himself entirely of his personality, and only when he is freed from all 'attributes' does he enjoy complete well-being.

To be able to criticize our impulses and instincts, we must take a standpoint that is beyond and behind them. "We should have to take up a position outside life, in order to be allowed to touch the problem of the value of life generally." (*Gōtzendāmmerung*). The Buddha's *anattā*-idea provides just this position and reveals the point from which we can shake to its foundations the entire phenomenal world with all its life, impulses and instincts. For this *anattā*-idea brings us logically and with intuitive perception to the awareness that in our very depths we stand beyond all these factors. We see that they are as inessential as they are inadequate. The more we detach ourselves from them, the more peaceful and the happier we become. Asked Seneca, "Do you regard as poor or as godlike the man who has freed himself from everything casual and fortuitous ?" Compare this with Udāna 1 : 1 : "Truly when things disclose themselves to the devout and faithful Brahmin with contemplative vision, all doubts then vanish from him, for he recognizes the reality that is bound up with causality."

What a man is or has already, cannot be willed or desired by him. Invariably we can will only something which we have and are not already; which is essentially foreign to us. As all that we can desire brings us suffering and is, in consequence, inadequate to us, and all unhappiness and misfortune come to us from without, it is wise to withdraw into ourselves in complete desirelessness and self-contentedness.

We are happiest when alone and freed from everything we have 'attributed' to ourselves. This is the application of metaphysical wisdom to practical life. The Self, no longer lost in cognition of the external world, returns to itself, and thus conceives everything else as Not-Self, as if non-existent.

As is obvious from the *anattā*-idea, the nothingness is the tabernacle of the most holy, of our own essence, thus of the world-ground, and so of God. Yet men are afraid of letting themselves fall into this nothingness.

Others, besides the Buddha, have seen the truth of this. Said Goethe, "We all suffer from life; in this your nothing I hope to find the all." And, "Our whole conjuring trick consists in our giving up our existence in order to exist." Schopenhauer also said, "Since all willing is error, the last work of intelligence is to abolish willing, whose aims and ends it had hitherto served. Accordingly, even the most perfect intelligence possible can be only a transition stage to that which no knowledge can ever reach."[1]

Dying, then, is simply the abandonment of the 'attribute' of the body and thus of the entire personality. Whoever detaches himself from his personality during his lifetime, dies before death. For him the physical death merely seals the detachment and his going over into the 'absolute state', as the Buddha defines the situation. In the 49th sutta of the *Majjhima-Nikāya* Brahma is made to say of his heaven : "But I, good sir, say 'permanent' because it is permanent, I say 'stable' because it is stable, I say 'eternal' because it is eternal . . . . : This is just what I say : This is not born, it does not age, it does not die, it does not pass away, it does not uprise; and because there is not another further escape, I say, there is not another further escape."[2]

1. Schopenhauer, *The World as will and Idea.* vol. 2, p. 610.
2. Translated by J.B. Horner.

But where there is the perishable and impermanent, there can be only pain and suffering. This, which was so clearly perceived by the Buddha, has been well understood by others. Said Schopenhauer : "whoever hopes to assuage the suffering of the pressure of the will through the satisfaction thereof, in that he secures the fulfilment of every desire, whereupon there at once arises a new desire, and hence a new pain demanding relief, resembles a man who cures the separate symptoms of venereal disease whose source is the virus he carries within himself, whereupon a fresh and worse symptom ensues." He added : "But the man who suppresses the will within himself and who, instead of hoping for alleviation and peace from objects, stops the source of evil, namely the will which alone gives objects the power to disturb his peace, resembles one who destroys the virus itself."

Again : "whoever tries to measure the happiness of life according to pleasures and delights, has taken a false standard. For pleasures are and remain negative .... Pain, on the other hand, is felt positively; and so its absence is the standard of happiness .... It follows from this that we should never purchase pleasure at the price, or even the risk, of pain, since we then pay what is positive and real for something that is negative and illusory. On the other hand, we are left with a gain when we sacrifice pleasures in order to avoid pain .... It is really the greatest absurdity to turn this scene of woe and lamentation into a pleasure-resort and to aim at joys and pleasures, rather than at the greatest possible freedom from pain .... For all pleasures are illusory."

Also : " .... experience after a time teaches us that happiness and pleasure are a *Fata Morgana* which is visible only from a distance and vanishes when we approach it ...."[1] Every pleasure rests on an illusion. All at once the object of pleasure is in reality not at all as we see it; and this applies above all to the human body as the cause of the keenest pleasure in voluptuousness.[2] Suffering, however, rests on the disappearance of the illusion, and hence on *disillusionment*, and it must inevi-

1. Schopenhauer, *Parerga* and *Paralipomena*, vol. 1, Aphorisms on the Wisdom of Life, chapter V.
2. See Grimm's *Botschaft des Buddha*, p. 82.

tably follow the pleasure "as the wheel follows the hoof of the ox that draws the cart".[1]

The majority of men and the majority of philosophers regard their stay in the phenomenal world as something to be extolled. They resign themselves to the overwhelming suffering of the phenomenal world, believing that, although they do not know what it is, there is a world plan, an end purpose to be reached in and with the phenomenal world. It does not seem to occur to them that this phenomenal world *in itself* might be the consequence of error and not of a wise plan, since in the *in-itself everything* is possible. Thus, from the first, it is an *arbitrary* assumption which at every step flies in the face of harsh reality. By ultimately destroying *everything* again and again, it announces most clearly that nothing has a value that extends beyond itself.

In general there are plans and purpose only *within* the phenomenal world, just as only *within* it are there beginnings. Everything in the world has a beginning, but the world itself has no beginning. No one has ever seen a thing originate from nothing. New things always manifest themselves as changes in things already existing. In the same way, everything *in* the world has a purpose, insofar as it is destined to bring about a new change within the world. But the world itself has no ultimate purpose. Even the concept of purpose is immanent and never transcendent.

The materialist is aware of this. The Marxist can point to nothing but flux and change. He detects no underlying ground of being. It is the same with the scientist. C. Oppermann, the physiologist and chemist describes the changes in the human body in great detail : "The vital processes bring about a constant deterioration and disintegration of the living substance, and this we summarize as wear and tear. The events in the change of substance, which aim at the replacement of the losses in living substance accruing in this way, are a principal task of the change in structural substance in adults. The nearer the youthful organism approaches the end of its development, the greater becomes, relatively, the part played by the change of building substance, which aims at the re-

1. *Dhammapada*, 1.

placement of worn-out tissue ... there also perishes from day to day under (similar) physiological conditions an equally large amount of living substance; hence the constant business of elimination."[1]

As Anton Kerner von Marilaun says, "This transformation proceeds every moment through the cells imperceptibly ....[2] The used-up elements of the cells are, with the break-up into their end-products, flushed by the blood from the tissues and, for the purpose of elimination, are directed into special organs. At the same time, the reparation for the elements that are used up is extracted from the blood, since the constituents of this, especially also the blood corpuscles themselves, are, with their destruction as such, worked up into the new cellular components ...."

In the *Sutta-Nipāta*, V.874 there is the reminder that our body is destroyed for us if we no longer behave as perceivers. "For on perception is based that which is called world-extension." It also says in the *Dhammapada*, V.254 : "The multitude delight in world-extension; the non-extenders of the world are the Perfect Ones." This simply means that the multitude delight in the subjective process of extending which occurs in the act of cognition, whereas the Perfect Ones abandon the entire process of cognition.

The religious view of the physical was provided by Saint Bernard : "Always bear in mind this triad : What were you ? An evil-smelling seed! What are you ? A vessel full of filth ! What will you be ? Food for worms ! If you consider carefully what comes out of your mouth, your nose, and through the other outlets of your body, you have never seen a more loathsome muck-heap ...."[3] The Monk Adam was equally forthright : "Do you not know that you desire to hold a painted and made-up mantle, when you look at a woman with lustful eyes ? Do you not see that what pleases you illicitly and seems to you to be something beautiful, harbours something that stinks ? When you crave to hold lustfully in your arms a graceful and pretty

1. G. Oppermann, *Biochemie*, volume 6, p. 205.
2. *Plant Life* revised by Prof. Dr. Hansen.
3. See the Latin original in K. E. Neumann's *Langere Sammlung*, note 694 to the 22nd discourse.

woman, you are wanting to hold a silk bag full of excrements."[1]

It must be mentioned that, according to the Buddha, were the body as intrinsically beautiful as it appears to be, it would still form a part of the world's illusion and so remain an integral source of suffering. It is not necessary to make out that matter has unpleasant aspects in order to demonstrate that it cannot, under any circumstances, satisfy the Self. That is satisfied only by detachment, and any link with the physical is attachment.

The reader may be disturbed by the claim that the material had no beginning, and he might well be asking how matter received its first impulse to move. In his *Naturphilosophie*, Euken says: "Motion has existed from all eternity and originates in the world not in a mechanical way through thrust, but dynamically. We can imagine the primordial state of matter as rest; or motion is the original state, and then rest is impeded motion. Both assumptions are logical, but it is infinitely more probable that motion is the primordial state, since rest describes only *one* instance of the spatial relations of matter, whereas motion can describe an infinite number of cases .... Rest (within the world) is by no means inactivity, but an actual opposition between two motions; thus there is not an absolute rest. As all forces are forces of motion, and a matter without force is inconceivable, action, motion, must be the original state of matter. Therefore motion must be included in the definition of matter."

Matter can, of course, be grasped positively. But the Self can only be given negative definition. "The body is not the Self, sensation is not the Self, perception is not the Self, activities of the mind are not the Self, consciousness is not the Self. What is seen, thought, heard, known and investigated in the mind is not the Self. The entire world is not the Self."

The Self, in fact, is a stranger in the world. Even the state that is absolutely adequate to us can be made clear only negatively, and in the end the path to it is a great and unique negation. Thus all the factors of the world and the entire world itself must be given up. It is this negation of all that seems to be positive to normal cognition which provides the almost insuperable obstacle to the understanding of the Buddha's doctrine by persons of average intelligence. But the scholarly as well as the un-

1. Johannes Bühler, *Klosterleben des Mittelalters*, pp. 183 *et seq.*

scholarly have identified their Self with their personality. Saccaka, "a practised dialectician", said in the 15th *sutta* of the *Majjhima-Nikāya*, in contradicting the Buddha : "Gotama, I certainly say : "The body is my Self, sensation is my Self, perception is my Self, activities of the mind are my Self, consciousness is my Self, and those crowds also say the same thing." The mystics have also used the word Self in this generally accepted sense. Their real Self, and hence what the Indian describes as Ātman or Attā, is called by them the primary ground and thus of the world itself.

The Buddha did not adopt this view. Consequently he was saved from falling into many of the errors which plague the West. The East asserts of its wisdom that it is the standard for all men at all times. Thus it applies even to the men of our day with their highly developed civilization and their complex technologies. In the wisdom of the Buddha there is no developing revelation. This distinguishes it sharply both from Christianity and from Western science. Christianity rests its claim to acceptance upon the assertion that it is a historical revelation which unfolded through the centuries. Christianity, no matter what its interpretation — and there are thousands of these — asserts that it is a supernatural revelation that took place in history.

Western science is certainly an evolutionary process, a constant deepening and widening of knowledge. With such a background, it is difficult for the European to see Buddhism as anything more than a piece of ancient wisdom which has value only because of its historical interest. Thus the European fails to test its content of truth. He appreciates it as no more than a historical phenomenon in the intellectual life of mankind. It is overlooked that the wisdom of the East differs from Christianity in one crucial respect. Its findings are not based on supernatural revelation which, ultimately, come into conflict with reality, and so show themselves to be in need of improvement. On the contrary, Buddhism asserts that its findings are the product of a normal but penetrating intuitive perception and reflection.

Thus its instruments of search and discovery are open to all men at all times, for they are common to all men. Thus, too, it is timeless, being valid for all men and all times, and is a truth which is incapable of further improvement. It does not demand belief. Rather it requires that nothing should be accepted on mere faith. The teaching calls for unbiased examination and objective valuation as does, say, the theorem of Pythagoras, which likewise cannot be assessed and disposed of as a mere product of history.

By appealing to knowledge and not belief, the East has rendered its teaching inaccessible to the great majority of people. An appeal to belief, irrational in itself and supported by absurd legends, would have resulted in widespread acceptance. Only a small minority are able to develop an independent intellectual approach in matters of religion. Schopenhauer described knowing as, "the most difficult organic function". The author of that intriguing book, *Ecclesiastes*, said, "much study is a weariness of the flesh", and an African tribe expressed the conviction of the vast majority of men in its proverb, "Thinking is the most terrible thing". Few indeed are those who seek truth for its own sake. Few, too, are those, even in those countries where popular education has conferred literacy on the masses, who pursue knowledge unless it promises material rewards.

In the spheres of politics and science most men are well content to accept authority, and there is a reverence for the modern 'expert' that is on a similar level to the respect once accorded witch doctors. In the province of religion, the respect for authority is boundless, allowing the professionals to propagate the most obvious and absurd ideas without challenge from the faithful.

The Buddha began his search for truth because of his realisation that the natural state of the human being was one of wretchedness and anguish. It is a belief that has been shared by men of towering intellectual stature. Socrates said flatly, "Life is terrible". Homer exclaimed, "Best of all things upon earth, not to be born, nor to behold the splendours of the sun." Aristotle stated, "Nature is devilish, not divine." Euripides claimed, "No one on the globe is happy." Crantor, who studied under Xenocrates, made the famous utterance, "..., from the earliest times has the lot of man been deplored by many very wise men. They regarded life as a penance, and likewise the birth of a man as the greatest misfortune."

Petrarch said, "This life seems to me to be a labyrinth of errors, a terrible desert, a muddy pool, a breathing death, a hell already in our lifetime, a long funeral procession." Thomas a Kempis claimed, "Truly is life on earth an affliction." Thomas Nashe described life as, "Brutish, nasty and short." Goethe said, "We all suffer from life." Schiller asked, "What man enjoyed life who looked into its depths?" Eduard v. Hartmann was constrained to say, "The native soil of the need for religion, the pessimistic view of the world, will continue to extend, for the more use men make of the means to earthly ease and comfort, the more are they bound to see how impossible it is to overcome in this way the pain and anguish of life, and to attain happiness or even only contentment." At the end of his life, Voltaire stated, "Happiness is only a dream, and pain is real. I have experienced it for eighty years." Yet Voltaire was highly favoured by nature and good fortune.

The improvements achieved by modern science in the spheres of health, hygiene, travel and diversion, the lifting of poverty and the extending of the life span in the twentieth century have made no difference to the pessimism of the acute observer. There is not only the gloomy view of existence expressed by such international figures as Aldous Huxley, T.S. Eliot, Wystan Auden and George Orwell, as well as a host of others, but the Irish playwright, Sean O'Casey, said to have written in *Juno And The Paycock* the greatest play of the last fifty years, took his generation of writers to task for their pessimism about life and living. Schopenhauer would have profoundly disagreed with him, for he was convinced that optimism is not only absurd, but a *wicked* way of thinking, a bitter mockery of the unspeakable sufferings of man.

The suggestion that the East's pessimism leads to a *transcendental optimism* is of no avail. Such pessimism, in other words, is like that with which the addict of morphia reproaches his doctor, because the latter tries to break him of his disastrous habit.

Is happiness, then, an illusion, mirage ? A simple woman of the world when asked what she would like as her eternal happiness after death replied, "I should like to have my peace and rest." This woman understood the essence of true happiness. For as long as restlessness, uneasiness and dissension prevail in a man, so long is he unhappy, just so long must he suffer. As the Buddha says: "Wherever inner peace is wanting, there is suffering."

Inner peace is wanting, and restlessness prevails in the human being when he is agitated by a wish that is not fulfilled, for every unsatisfied wish is a torment. All human beings—indeed all beings generally—seek to satisfy their desires in order to be delivered from the inner anguish which is prompted by their unsatisfied desires.

Why have men so many desires ? Because their present state and circumstances are unsuitable to them; they are inadequate to their innermost nature. They still need something—indeed, they need a great deal—in order that they might say, "I am in a state which is wholly adequate to me; I am now perfectly satisfied with my state and wholly happy in it."

The creatures of this world so lack this state that Meister Eckhart could say, "All beings bear bitterness within themselves." It is clear that, if we were in a state *perfectly* adequate to ourselves, we would no longer desire anything. In fact, were we to ask a being enjoying a state that was wholly adequate to him what he still desired, he would answer: "Desire? What is that ?"

If no desire at all arises in a man, there he is not agitated by inner restlessness, as every inner restlessness or discord is a restlessness of the *will.* Said Meister Eckhart, "All the discord of passions and fury comes solely from our own will, whether or not we realise it." Thus, were we in a state altogether suitable to us, we should be free of all desire and there would dwell in us perfect peace. "The man who has all his wants and desires has peace," said Eckhart.

Perfect Happiness, perfect desirelessness, perfectly suitable state and perfect inner peace are identical concepts. Conversely, where there is desire, a will, there must be an inadequate state to be overcome.

As this overcoming is not achieved, as the will is constantly thwarted and frustrated, beings are subjected to inner discord and hence to suffering. All willing and, consequently, all suffering are merely symptoms of an inadequate situation. In a wholly suitable state not even the trace of willing or suffering is possible.

Is it possible for the human being to achieve such a state, in which, to all eternity, no further desire could arise? Is there, in fact, a perfect, absolute happiness to which beings can advance? This is the primary problem of all existence. Is it possible to solve this basic problem ? However large the claim may sound, this crucial problem is very easy to answer.

The desire for a wholly adequate state is the deepest longing of every human heart. As long as a being has not yet attained this state of absolute happiness, he is not satisfied. Consequently, he finds no peace or rest. He must continue to struggle to achieve statisfaction. Only a being who could state, "Now I am *perfectly* content", is free of all desire, and so has ceased to struggle and strive.

The absolutely adequate state is really the deepest and ultimate desire of all beings. And a primary longing common to all beings must be able to find fulfilment. For the deepest and ultimate purposes of nature are always achieved by her, although only after immeasurable periods of time. Nature works along the line of least resistance; and creates no needs which cannot be fully satisfied. Therefore, the deepest need, the primary longing for a perfectly happy and adequate state, must be met above all others. Beings would not have this primary longing if it were incapable of fulfilment. If we have not yet discovered the path to this final and ideal state, the fault lies in our own weakness, not in objective reality.

This longing for an absolutely adequate state is the primary *impulse* of all beings and springs from the deepest recesses of reality which is not illuminated by any cognition. It is in this realm that every existing thing has its roots, and in which for this very reason the meaning of all that exists is included. This primary impulse is at the same time recognized as the artless, and also unambiguous, proclaimer of the ultimate destiny of beings.

As such, it cannot reach peace until the goal of the wholly adequate state is attained, even though world-periods may be needed for this. It is the whip which scourges beings incessantly and untiringly in this direction. Conversely, if the primary impulse is extinguished in a being and he thus reaches peace, this means that he has attained the absolutely adequate state and has fulfilled his destiny. As Laotse said : "To have arrived at peace means to have fulfilled one's destiny." He added : "To have fulfilled one's destiny means to be in keeping with the eternal order, and to know how to be in keeping with the eternal order means to be perfect and complete."

These words mean that the eternal order is that one in which every being finds himself in a state wholly adequate to himself.

Only in such an order is there no change and so is eternal. Such an order corresponds to the mental picture every man carries within himself of the eternal order. As long as this order is disturbed, disorder and confusion flourish. During this confusion, the eternal order strives to eliminate this disturbance. It protests, laments and threatens by way of conscience after every deed that is opposed to it. And it blesses by way of a good conscience every action that lies in the direction of the absolutely adequate state. When a person has reached this state the herald of the eternal order, the primary impulse, is silenced. Such a 'Perfect One', free of all urges and promptings, knows boundless peace and absolute happiness. Indeed, he has fulfilled his destiny. A state altogether adequate to us is contained within the Eternal Order. Thus its realization is not only possible, but is precisely the real task of our lives. Kant expressed this in the words, "You can, for you ought."

Of course, this state is not to be realized on earth. For on earth, apart from everything else, death reigns as a natural and universal law. And in a state that was perfectly adequate, there could be neither death nor dying. For what perfection could there be in a state in which there would always be the awareness : "Now I feel perfectly happy, but soon the whole grandeur and splendour will be no more, for I must die. As a German poet said, "Ah, what makes us happy would have to be permanent."

As the state that is perfectly adequate to us must be innocent of death and dying, it must be situated outside the earth and thus be in a different realm. Because of this, the man who wishes to be in permanent possession of the wholly adequate state, must emigrate to that other realm. This can be achieved only when we discard our present body.

Here we encounter two entirely new problems. That of our immortality and the question as to whether there is another realm at all into which we can pass. Happily, these two problems are already solved for the man who has followed our discourse with full understanding. It is certain that our longing for a perfectly adequate state cannot be deceptive. It is equally certain that this state cannot be realized on earth. For these reasons it is certain that we are not annihilated by death. There must, therefore, be another realm in which the state wholly adequate to us can be reached.

Of course, so-called science suggests that man is annihilated in death. But the vast majority of men are not disconcerted by this suggestion. They lean confidently on the infallibility of their *fundamental feeling*, of their *primary instinct*, which affirms to them again and again : "Your longing for a perfect, and thus immortal, state of happiness must be capable of perfect satisfaction, and as it cannot be satisfied on earth, it must be fulfilled in another world." Inspired by that fundamental feeling, that primary instinct, man confides in the religions which tell him about the perfectly happy state in a kingdom of heaven. He confides in them even when they cannot demonstrate to him his immortality and that kingdom of heaven. His faith in this everlasting kingdom finds unshakeable support in the fundamental longing and feeling of man himself.

The great question which must occur to all except the dullest intellect is : "What is the ultimate purpose, the final goal, of all our activity ? Why are we in the world ?" The man who gave a clear and unequivocal answer to this question was the Buddha, the one who awakened from dreaming (=*suttappabuddha*)[1]. He defined mankind as "... beings who crave for happiness."

We are in this world only because we wish to be happy. Any other reason is illusive. In all that we do or fail to do, in all that we think and plan, we are looking for happiness. Indeed, we are looking for complete and perfect happiness. But this would mean realizing the state that is absolutely adequate and appropriate to us, the state in which no further desire could ever occur. As long as we have not attained this complete happiness, so long do we find no rest or peace. We continue to strive and struggle for that state. Had we attained it, all desire would be permanently extinguished in us, and we would be free of the torment of unrest and anxiety. Therefore, we seek not merely happiness, but perfect and permanent happiness. This cannot be ours as long as we are afflicted by suffering in any form. Man may possess everything he desires, but if the least pain disturbs him, even the fear of future suffering, then he is not *perfectly* happy. Thus the Buddha

1. *Saṁ. Nik.* 1, p. 143; VI, 1, 4.

offers the complete definition : "We are beings who crave for happiness and dislike suffering."[1]

For every being in the world the dominant factor is suffering. Thus everyone sees his immediate aim as liberation from the suffering that threatens or oppresses him. But what is suffering ? It is thwarted desire, impeded will. We suffer when a wish cannot be immediately satisfied. Frustration causes restlessness and anxiety. "Where inner peace is wanting, there suffering exists."[2] This being the case, every being is bent on satisfying his desires. No one can endure indefinitely the agonizing unrest of unfulfilled desire.

We try to procure those objects—money, fame, a wife and family—to which we are drawn by our desires. Life is a perpetual struggle for the 'good things' of the world. But it is impossible to satisfy desire in this way. Few gain the things they desire, for few know the answer to the question, *How much is enough* ? But even those who gain all they set their hearts on winning, cannot escape suffering. All things are transient. They must separate from us or we must separate from them. This anguish of transitoriness is associated with all earthly existence. To be in the world means to occupy space ; and what occupies space is material. As all matter is in a state of constant change, all things are transitory. It is impossible for a single being in the entire universe to acquire the objects of his desire and thereby escape suffering. But it is, of course, an axiom as well as a platitude that whoever is looking for happiness is looking for it in the wrong place.

Nevertheless, it must also be axiomatic that it must be possible to satisfy the primary longing of the human heart. The fulfilment of the ultimate longing of all beings for a state absolutely adequate to them must really be possible, for this longing would not exist if it could not be satisfied. Said E. v. Feuchtersleben, "What we strive for with all our might comes to us, for longing is only an expression of what is in conformity with our true being." If we have not found the way to this ideal state, the fault lies with ourselves and not with objective reality. Indeed, the right path is automatically

1. *Majjh. Nik.*, 94th sutta.
2. *Saṁ. Nik.*, V, p. 398; LV, 40.

opened up to the one who recognizes as wrong the path usually taken to happiness—that of *satisfying* the will. The right path must be freedom from suffering. Perfect happiness does not exist where suffering is felt ; that is, where anything can still be willed. To find the possibility of happiness, we must advance beyond all suffering and so beyond all willing.

As all suffering is simply the anguish which results from the nonsatisfaction of a wish, from the frustration of a will, all suffering can be eradicated by annihilating desire and willing. In fact, this is the only way to annihilate suffering, for only in this way is the source of suffering eradicated. The path to perfect happiness is that of complete desirelessness. The nearer the approach to happiness, the nearer we approach a desireless state. "The man who abandons all sensual pleasures and wanders away without desire, without self-conceit, and without egoism attains peace."

From time immemorial detachment has been the path taken by all sages, in the West as well as in the East. There is an almost embarrassing choice of literature from the many who have turned their backs on the world in their search for contentment. Aristotle maintained that "the sage aspires to painlessness and not to pleasure." Socrates, one of the greatest, offered as the highest ideal "to need nothing".

The Cynics went even further than Socrates. The founder of their school, Antisthenes, a disciple of Socrates, like his master, wore a shabby cloak, like those worn by peasants, and he was the first in the West to carry the knapsack as the symbol of destitution and the staff as the symbol of homelessness. He taught that the surest way to happiness is to have no wants. Such a frame of mind, he claimed, brought supreme bliss and is, therefore, the true task of our lives. He went on to say that, once discovered, such a state could not be lost, for he who has once experienced the blissful feeling of detachment from all possessions and all concern about them, will never again surrender it. Such a man recognizes that it is "better to be insane than lustful and voluptuous."

Diogenes, the most famous of the pupils of Antisthenes, carried frugality to such extremes that he was called Socrates gone mad. He lived in a tub and drank from a wooden vessel. But when he saw a boy drinking water from his hollowed hands, Diogenes was so ashamed, he threw away the vessel.

The Stoics pursued the same path, and they had their followers and imitators in all countries. Even a few Roman Emperors were Stoics. They sought happiness on the path of frugality. They declared that, just as a stick is either straight or crooked, so every human action is either good or bad. Actions are good, they said, when actions are controlled by reason; bad when they are inspired by passion. The man who possesses the one virtue of having no wants or needs has all the virtues, as they all spring from wisdom as their common source. Whoever does not follow the voice of his reason, but is ruled by his passions, is to be regarded as out of his senses. There are four chief emotions from which all passions spring : pleasure and pain, desire and fear; and all four are diseases of the soul. The physician who cures them is the *sage*.

Everyone capable of thinking logically will acknowledge the cogency of these claims. They are likely to feel admiration for those able to muster the Socratic strength of will to act in accordance with this wisdom. But Socrates, the Cynics and Stoics, in common with all who have taken the way of detachment, have only begun to tread the path. They are subject to the suffering associated with individuality. Even they must endure the pains of illness, or growing old mentally and physically, and the anguish of death. Only when these three drastic forms of suffering are forever blocked, can perfect freedom from suffering be attained, and permanent happiness be procured. Yet who would presume to have the ability to bring this about ?

In spite of all apparent impossibility, man certainly believes in the possibility of overcoming these factors of suffering. Indeed it is in the promise of such a conquest that the value of religion is to be found. The question is whether in this life we can realize the conquest of death and thus, of course, of sickness and old age, so that we know ourselves to be *beyond the reach of death* and intuitively perceive ourselves to be immortal. From time immemorial all wisdom seems to have failed in this respect. Nevertheless, this is what the Buddha has to say :

"Give care, O monks, the deathless has been attained. I

will instruct you, I will impart to you the doctrine. Following my instructions, ye shall know and realize that utmost noble goal of the holy life (namely immortality) for yourselves even in this present lifetime."

The solution to the problem of mortality, however, was only one side of the problem. The ultimate goal of the Buddha is neither more nor less than an advance to the state that is wholly adequate to us, and so to a state of perfect happiness. The Buddha describes as "the incomparable condition of supreme peace", and also as "what is adequate" that state in which in all eternity there cannot arise any desire for change or for another state to replace it. It is a state in which boundless peace prevails, for a want of peace is always a restlessness of the will. In that same *sutta* he expressly declares that the attainment of this final state was the aim of his aspiration, and that, in fact, he reached this goal as "the state of perfect security", "free from birth and old age, from sickness, death, care and defilement."

The end of this goal is also freedom from suffering. Indeed, according to the Buddha, there is absolutely nothing more to be done but to render ourselves free from suffering, since in the annihilation of suffering is removed the obstacle which bars the way to the state of supreme happiness. The path of the Buddha ends in the annihilation of suffering. "As before so also now, I preach only Suffering and the Cessation of Suffering." Because suffering culminates in death, he often speaks of the "attainment of deathlessness" or "immortality" as tantamount to the conquest of suffering. In his wish to liberate himself from suffering, he wished "to pass over into deathlessness," "to get beyond the reach of death". Therefore his problem amounted to the annihilation of all factors that create suffering, and especially those that condition death, *without his being annihilated himself in the process.* For if he were annihilated along with the factors that create suffering, then this would not be "liberation" or "deliverance", such less would it be the attainment of the "state of perfect peace" and of "complete and perfect security." It would be nothing better than eternal death.

Accordingly the Buddha faced two questions :

1. What factors in us cause and make us subject to death ?

2. Are these factors essentially connected with us so that their annihilation entails our own annihilation, or are they not essential components of ours so that their annihilation does not affect ourselves ? Only in this case, of course, would "liberation" from them be possible.

Answering the first question presupposed the analysis of the whole personality. The personality consists of the material body, sensations, perception, activities of the mind, and consciosuness. There are six forms of consciousness—visual, auditory, olfactory, gustatory, tactile and mental. The activity of consciousness assumes the form of sensation and then of perception, with the result that there occurs in the organ of thought the activity of thinking about what is sensed and perceived, and there comes to life a whole host of mental activities. The four groups of sensation, perception, activities of thought, and consciousness, are caused and conditioned by the bodily organism. If a sense-organ becomes incapable of function, the corresponding sensations and perceptions fail to appear. If the organ of thought as the central organ is seriously damaged, then all consciousness is at an end. Therefore the bodily organism with its six organs of sense is the six-senses machine which generates consciousness.[1]

As it is the transitory quality of life which produces suffering, all these groups are examined, and they are found to be transitory. In this the Buddha was in conformity with the conclusions of presentday science. In his On the State of Mind of the Dying, Professor L.R. Muller states, "Science is not able to visualize the soul's survival without a brain." Thus there can be no independent mind that could survive the disintegration of the body. This being so, the entire personality is transient and so, with the advent of this transitoriness, it brings us suffering. "The body is transient, sensation and perception are transient, activities of the mind are transient, cognition is transient."

This, then, for the Buddha was the solution to the first of the two questions. From this it follows that the annihilation

1. Cf. Grimm, *The Doctrine of the Buddha*, Akademie Verlag Berlin (ET), 1958, pp. 67-91.

of *all* suffering is possible only through the annihilation of the entire personality, and hence of sensing and perceiving, of the whole emotional life, and of all consciousness.

It would seem that the second question is already answered. That we cannot free ourselves from suffering without annihilating ourselves. If nothing except these five groups of personality can be found in us, their annihilation must inevitably necessitate our own. Indeed, this result is actually arrived at by all philosophical systems which recognize that our entire consciousness, and thus all sensation and mental activity are merely functions of the body, which is the apparatus of consciousness. But, in point of fact, the Buddha succeeded in wholly detaching himself at will from all the elements of his personality, from all sensation and consciousness, and then, after some days, in returning to them again.[1]

Consequently, through deep religious and practical experience, there was established for him the fact that all the elements of our personality are not essentially bound up with us *and that their elimination leaves us untouched.* What is more, as one perfectly awakened, he was able by reflection to convey into the logical thought-forms of reason, and so to render accessible and intelligible to others, the experience and insight gained from the highest contemplative vision. This he did in an astonishingly simple manner and perfect clarity in the following syllogism :

1. Major premise :
   "What I see arise and pass away and, in consequence of this transitoriness, brings me suffering, cannot be myself."
2. Minor premise :
   "I now see all the five groups of my personality constantly arise and pass away and, with their passing, bring me suffering."
3. Conclusion :
   "Therefore all of them are not my Self."

In keeping with its immense importance, the Buddha repeats this syllogism again and again. Of each of the five groups of our personality, he always states that it is transi-

1. See especially the 111th *sutta* of the *Majjhima-Nikāya*.

tory and therefore full of suffering, and he deduces the conclusion that "what is changeable is to be regarded by the really wise as 'not belonging to me, this am I not, this is not my Self."

The result of the Great Syllogism is the *anattā*-idea. *An-attā* (*attā* is the Pāli form of the Sanskrit word *ātman*, the Self), means literally *not the Self*. It is simply the condensation of the words, 'this belongs to me not, this am I not, this is not my Self'. "What is transient is full of suffering; what is full of suffering is *anattā*; what is *anattā* is something to which the following words apply : 'This belongs to me not, this am I not, this is not my Self'."

The Buddha saw that everything corporeal, all sensation, perception, all activities of the mind, all cognition—in fact, the entire personality—are *anattā*, not the Self. The earnest seeker capable of understanding these words is shown the course he has to take. The first flash brings an unexpected joy. "This doctrine is joyful in its beginning .... " In cognitive contemplation the *anattā*-idea becomes more and more *anattā*-wisdom which gives perfect security and cannot be shaken by anything. Thus the Dhammapada v. 97 says that he who grasps the *anattā*-idea no longer needs to believe in the eternal. He achieves it. "Whoever no longer needs to believe, but knows the uncreated, he truly is the exalted among men."

According to the Buddha, this *anattā*-idea is something unprecedented, something quite unique, which no one except a perfectly Awakened one can discover. The factors of personality exhaust the entire world, and no one has ever discovered in it anything other than the five elements of personality. Because of this, they form the whole of the actual and possible content of our consciousness and thus of that which is knowable. In the five groups of our personality we experience the world. Therefore, according to the Buddha, this entire world, everything cognizable, is without any reservation not our Self. Thus, in itself, the Self is supramundane, and so it also wholly withdrawn from cognition.

The *anattā*-wisdom gained in cognitive contemplation forms the unshakeable foundation of the Buddha's teaching. All the other parts are simply the logical consequences of this. To one capable of understanding the *anattā*-idea and for whom this comprehension gives direction to his thoughts, words and deeds, the Buddha's whole teaching is thus soon withdrawn from the conflict of opinions. Every exposition and estimation of the Buddha's doctrine must always be an exposition and appreciation of the *anattā*-idea, of the spiritual need giving rise to it and of the resultant train of thought.

It would be unreasonable to expect that the irrefutable correctness of this idea will at once be obvious to the reader, even if he has a gift for metaphysics. It is too remote from the realms of ordinary thought for this. Moreover, the tendency to regard personality as essential to us—even as our essence—is too deeply engrained in us for thought not to be coloured by it.

The *anattā*-idea opens up the possibility of freeing ourselves from all the factors of personality which produce suffering and thus of freeing ourselves from suffering itself. This clears the way to perfect happiness. But the price—which must be paid in advance—for this happiness is high. It is nothing less than one's own personality, the entire world, itself. But this is a small price to pay for perfect happiness. For all the pleasures of the world are, as Schopenhauer saw, under sentence of death. Whoever wills them affirms life and thus affirms death also.

According to the *anattā*-idea, no factor of personality and thus nothing of the world is our Self. This does not mean that the Self dwells in immobility and immutability beyond personality. It merely means that the five groups of personality are not the Self, that they do not of necessity belong to the Self, and hence that their loss does not affect the Self. The Buddha says: "What does not belong to you, give up. What is given up will bring you blessings and well-being. And what does not belong to you? Bodily form, sensation, perception, activity of the mind, consciousness; give them up. The things given up by you will bring you blessings and well-being."[1]

For the rest, we are intimately bound up with our personality, "like a man who seizes a twig with hands covered with resin."[2] For this reason, the Buddha also calls the five

1. *Saṃ. Nik.*, XXII, 33.
2. *Aṅg. Nik.*, IV, 178.

groups of personality, "groups of grasping". That we grasp them is due to our will. "The five groups of grasping are rooted in the will." This will, in the form of a mighty thirst, as the Buddha says, stands behind personality. It is a will to shape and then to use the body in order (by means of its sense-organs) to produce the other four groups of personality, such as sensation, perception, thought activity, and consciousness, that the world might be perceived and enjoyed.

This relation between Self and will, on the one hand, and cognition, on the other, was also uncovered by Schopenhauer. "Cognition", he wrote, "is a mere function of the brain, and is not our real self. Our true self, the kernel of our true being, is that which is to be found behind this, and which really knows nothing but willing and not-willing, being contented and not contented, with all the modifications of the thing called feelings, emotions and passions. This it is which produces that other thing, which does not sleep with it when it sleeps, which also remains unimpaired when that other thing becomes extinct in death."[1]

Even this willing, this thirsting, is not necessarily connected with us. It is never an end in itself, but is the means to the attainment of a definite object which in the light of our cognition appears to be something pleasant and so worth desiring. All willing can aim only at something foreign and extraneous. For it is directed to things that are outside and not the Self.

Thirst or will also decides for us when we are compelled to abandon this body and to seize in another womb a fresh fertilized germ, and so form a new six-senses-apparatus. This grasping at a fresh germ must go on as long as we have, at the moment of our death, a will or thirst to remain connected with the world. In this way, we achieved our present body. We thirsted for a body and so grasped at the fertilized germ in the womb of our mother. This thirst arose through the use of a previous apparatus of cognition with which we had already perceived the world and had learnt to like it, a process which goes back into the endless past. The chain of our rebirths is closed; in its beginninglessness and possible

1. Schopenhauer, *The World as Will and Idea*, vol. 2, p. 239.

endlessness it is only a reflection of our own essence which is beyond all time.

The Buddha's doctrine of rebirth is not an article of faith. It is cogently and conclusively demonstrated. It is the corollary of the *anattā*-idea. It finds a clear echo in the words of Schopenhauer: "What does the loss of this individuality (personality) matter to me who carry within myself the possibility of innumerable individualities?"

Everything depends on our willing. It is this willing which ensnares us in becoming and consequently in suffering. Were we to desire nothing more, thirst for nothing more, all suffering would become impossible. We need only become desireless by discovering that the world and all that it contains is inadequate for us. Everything in it is transitory and so brings us suffering. Above all, we must lose all craving for our own body, as this is the apparatus by which we are tied to the world. In the absence of a will for this, we shall no longer seize any fresh germ at the hour of our approaching death. Thus no new body will be formed for us, nor any new organs of sense, and we shall for ever be delivered from this world of suffering. "These six senses will be entirely and completely abolished without any remainder, and nowhere and in no place will there again arise six other senses."[1]

But we have not yet got so far. For there still lives in us a will which has not been destroyed by all previous knowledge, and which, in fact, cannot be stifled thereby. The nobler a man is and the more aware is he of the truth of Jakob Bohme's words: "If all the mountains were books, and all the seas ink, and all the trees pens, they would still not suffice to describe all the pain in the world." Aware of this, he feels an ardent desire to free the entire world from suffering, and to convey his fellow-sufferers as well as himself into the absolutely adequate state. Yet this longing cannot be brought to extinction through a knowledge of its pernicious nature. On the contrary, it is, as everyone plainly feels, the noblest thing that can generally be roused in a being, indeed it is not of this world at all. For this world is organized on the principle of egosim. But that pain, excited by the suffering of others,

1. *Saṃ. Nik.*, 230: XLVIII, 53.

appears in us as compassion, and it breaks through egoism to such an extent that it can lead to the complete sacrifice of one individual for the sake of another. In the world the barriers of 'I' and 'you' prevail, but the will born of compassion demolishes them. This will, therefore, can spring only from the very depths of our real innermost essence to which nothing individual or personal reaches.

For, as the *anattā*-idea makes plain, the individual or the personal is not that innermost core, is not the Self. Therefore, in reality there is not the contrast between I and you, but only different personalities, different complexes of the five groups, with which, through ignorance, we identify ourselves. Are we, then, one in the very depths of our ultimate being? The *Vedānta* has answered this question in the affirmative. *Tat tvam asi*, it states, "Thou art that." This must remain mere speculation, for the essence of our nature cannot be reached by way of cognition. Cognition is directed wholly outwards, on to the world of the Not-Self. "The Self-Existent (the Ātman, the I) bored the cavities outwards, so that we see outwards, but not into the inner Self."[1] Tee Buddha, in complete conformity with things as they are, had to restrict himself to ascertaining what is not the Self, and so he acknowledges only the concept of the Not-Self, not that of the self. This brought him to the realization that his personality, neither in whole nor in part, was not his Self. But because he recognized that his personality was in no sense his Self, all the limitations imposed by his personality were broken down. And although it was not granted to him to penetrate by means of his cognition to his Self, he came to recognize himself as boundless. "A Perfect One freed from personality is deep, immeasurable, unfathomable, like the great ocean."

The result of this boundlessness of his true essence, which had now broken through "like a chicken through its egg-shell", was that, naturally, there was no longer for him the contrast between I and you, but "he dwelt as immeasurable as space."[2] Therefore, wherever there was suffering, he too was bound to suffer, and there inevitably arose in him the will to annihilate

1. *Kāṭhaka-Upaniṣad* IV, 1, 14.
2. *Sutta-Nipāta,* 1065.

suffering wherever it occurred. Every truly compassionate person walks in the steps of the Buddha, and he no longer identifies himself simply with his personality, but instinctively divines the illusory nature of the limits of his personality. Thus he is already numbered amongst the good in contrast to the egoists who are the bad. Between these two classes of persons exists an immeasurable gulf : "Distant are the clouds, distant are the valleys of the earth — far from the ocean is the other shore — yet further still than these, they say, are the good and bad kinds of men."

For the Buddha the problem of liberating himself from suffering became equated with the problem of liberating the entire world. He declares : "I then looked upon the world with a Buddha's eye. And I saw beings of a noble nature and of a common nature, sharp-witted and dull-witted, highly gifted and poorly endowed, quick of comprehension and dull of understanding, and those who think it dangerous to speak in glowing terms of another world."[1]

This will to save the world, however, could not arise in him, because he was bound to recognize at once the impossibility of such an undertaking. There cannot possibly arise any will for something that must be acknowledged to be impossible. No legless man can will to run a mile in four years, much less can he will to run a mile in less than four minutes. But the Buddha, who always addressed himself to the possible, was left with the problem of satisfying his ardent wish, born of his boundless compassion, to annihilate all suffering in the world insofar as that was possible. As this wish appeared to be justified, it could only be satisfied by being actually fulfilled. The Buddha fulfilled it because, during his lifetime, he showed "infinite kindness to all that lives and breathes." He thus did all that was possible for him to do. He satisfied his wish to eliminate the world's suffering to the limits of the possible. Beyond that, obviously, he could not go. The Buddha achieved the state in which there is no desire and in which there is complete freedom from suffering. In this sense he also formulated the ethic of the cultivation of immeasurable and boundless kindness. Because his compassion was without limit it em-

1. *Majjihma-Nikāya*, 85th. *sutta*.

braced not only all human beings, but also every living creature and even plants, "beings that have only one organ of sense." Absolute desirelessness becomes apparent primarily in respect of our own body as the apparatus for producing consciousness. Also as regards his body, the man without desire is wholly detached inwardly and so, even during his lifetime, he experiences detachment from his personality, since, in the *anattā*-view, he perceives intuitively that such personality is wholly foreign to him. Thus, while he is still alive, the following applies to him :

"If ignorance is finally abolished, there no longer exists the body in consequence of which there arises within himself pleasure and pain, there is no longer speech in consequence of which there arises within himself pleasure and pain, there is no longer mind in consequence of which there arise within himself pleasure and pain; there is no field, no object, no domain, no connection, in consequence of which there arises within himself pleasure and pain."[1] In the same work,[2] this *anattā*-view is described in the following words : "Not to speak of the present bodily forms, the past ones were perishable, brought suffering, were not the Self (*anattā*), and the future ones will be perishable, will bring suffering, will not be the Self. With such contemplative vision, the elect disciple loses interest (*anapekho hoti*) in the previous bodily form, does not look forward to the future bodily form, and attains to a weariness of and indifference to the present bodily form, to its elimination." And again : "The arising of bodily form, of sensation, of perception, of activities of the mind, of cognition, their existence and their manifestation — all this is the origination of suffering, the existence of diseases, the manifestation of old age and death. The disappearance of bodily form, of sensation, of perception, of activities of the mind, of cognition, their cessation, coming to rest and vanishing (*rūpassa nirodho vūpasamo atthagamo*)—all this is the cessation, coming to rest, and vanishing of suffering." Thus the one free of all bodily form, and all we understand by the term personality, is free from suffering. "Disappearance of the thirsting will is attained; the message of the Awakened One is fulfilled."[3]

1. *Sam. Nik.* II, 40: XII, 25.
2. *Ibid,* III, p. 19, 20, 31, 32: XII, 9, 10,11; 29, 30.
3. Nuns'Psalm.

Freedom from suffering is, of course, purely negative. What of the *perfect* happiness which the Buddha promises ? The gateway to perfect happiness is blocked by the rock of suffering. As soon as this rock is removed, the path is open to the final and ideal state. What is more, at the moment of complete freedom from suffering, we plunge into absolute happiness.

This is easy to understand. We desire, wish and crave only if we feel the lack of something. For a man who is unaware that he lacks anything, cannot long for anything. On the other hand, if he feels the need of something, then he is in a state of dissatisfaction and he is burdened by a sense of inadequacy. This state, however, is the universal one of all living creatures, and the higher their development, the more dissatisfied they are likely to feel, as they are almost certain to have more wants than creatures of a lower order. An animal is content if it is fed, watered and adequatly sheltered. But a human being requires much more to be content. Indeed, such is his nature that his reach exceeds his grasp. He feels the need of more than he can achieve. Thus he is in a state of permanent frustration, or in a state of inadequacy. In such a state the creature is umnappy and embittered. "All beings inwardly bear bitterness," said Meister Eckhart, and the human being, because his apparent needs and his wants are so numerous, and because he can foresee and so fret and fear, is, of all creatures, most burdened with bitterness.

This explains the perfectly logical claim that the willing, desiring and instinctive craving of beings are conditioned by the inadequacy of the circumstances in which they find themselves. And the human being finds himself in a situation in which, because it is foreign to his true nature, he cannot, strive how he may, find the joy and satisfaction he so earnestly craves. If all beings were in a situation which was wholly in accordance with their needs, then there could not possibly arise in them any desire nor even what we call instinctive craving. For desiring is not only not a property of our essence, any more than is instinctive craving, but, on the contrary, it is as repugnant to us as is our inadequate state. For this reason it gives rise to inward bitterness.

Willing and desiring are simply the symptoms of the frustrating situation in which we find ourselves. In the saint who has made himself wholly free from suffering, who has liberated himself from the entire phenomenal world (including his personality), there vanish completely those symptoms of the inadequate situation — willing, desiring, thirsting. The wholly adequate state has been attained. This is the state that is beyond the phenomenal world and in which no desire of any kind can ever again arise. This is expressed in the following equation :

Willing, desiring, thirsting
=an absence of something desired.

Absence of something desired
=suffering, inward bitterness, disharmony.

Suffering, inward bitterness
= a state of inadequacy.

Hence willing, desiring, thirsting
= a state inadequate to us.

Conversely, it follows that :
An absence of need or desire
or thirsting
=nothing is felt to be missing.

Nothing felt to be missing
= supreme contentment.

Supreme contentment
=a state perfectly adequate to us.

The above equations are not complete. All willing, desiring, instinctive craving signifies inner discord and dissension; every fulfilment of a wish or thirsting brings pleasure. But as all objects of desire are transitory, no fulfilment of a wish or craving can be permanent, all such pleasure is turned into bitterness and suffering. It is the final silencing of desire or thirsting which brings that inner contentment which widens to boundless peace; the state in which all thirsting and all desires have become dormant. Thus we have :

Willing, desiring, thirsting
=discord, disharmony.

Freedom from will, desire and thirsting
=peace, contentment.

Never again willing anything, desiring, thirsting
= eternal peace, perfect contentment.

Thus is established the following crystallization of the above equations :

Eternal peace
=perfectly adequate state.

It is now obvious why the Buddha declares the ultimate goal of all endeavour to be liberation from suffering. If all suffering is annihilated, then it is no longer possible to miss anything, for to miss anything would cause suffering. But when nothing at all is missed, then the adequate state has been achieved. Freedom from suffering, an adequate state and perfect happiness are identical concepts. "Those who are desireless and with vigorous minds stand firm in Gotama's teaching have won the greatest prize (*pattipatta*), have plunged into the deathless, and enjoy supreme peace."[1] "When things have reached full development, each returns to its origin. Returning to its origin means coming to rest. Coming to rest means having fulfilled its destiny. Having fulfilled its destiny means corresponding to the eternal order."[2] Because the Buddha was able to accord with the eternal order, (*Dhamma*), he rightly called himself a "Buddha", an Enlightened One, for "to know how to be in accord with the eternal order means to be enlightened", as Laotse said.

Since absolute desirelessness is perfect happiness, it surpasses infinitely any other kind of happiness. "Let there be a good youth, well read, prompt in action, steady in mind and strong in body. Let this whole earth be full of wealth for him. That is one human bliss."[3] The claim is then made that a

1. Su., V. 228.

2. Laotse, or Lao-Tze, a contemporary of confucius. His fame rests on the classic, *Tao-te-ching*.

3. *Taittiriya-Upaniṣad*, 11, 8. 1; an English translation by Radha-Krishnan is to be found in the *Principal Upanishads*, London 1953, pp. 550-551.

man well versed in the Vedas and not smitten by desire is a hundred times a human bliss, which is equal to one bliss of the fairies. A hundred times this bliss is the bliss of divine fairies, and a hundred times their bliss is that of the Fathers in their long enduring world. Further comparisons are made, until there are ten in all, each a hundred times greater than the one previously mentioned. It is then claimed : "And one hundred times that bliss (of Brahma) does not equal one measure of a great sage who is free from desires. . . . . . He who knows this (desireless state) reaches the SELF which consists of (naught but) bliss."

Again : ". . . by obtaining the reward of Brahman his fetters are cut asunder, he knows no hope, no fear from others as little as from himself, he knows no desires; and having attained imperishable, infinite happiness, he stands blessed in the true Brahman . . . . Freedom from desires is, as it were, the highest praise to be taken from the best treasure."[1]

The Buddha, however, says : "Whatever there is in sensuous well-being in the world and whatever there may be in such divine well-being, these are not a thousandth part of the well-being brought about by the annihilation of thirst (desirelessness)."[2] Over the entrance to true happiness glow in letters of fire the words : *Vivicc'eva kāmehi, vivvicca akusalehi dhammehi,* "Far from the pleasures evoked by the objects of the senses, far from those things that are pregnant with evil." There are no words to describe the happiness of perfect desirelessness, for it is ineffable. That is why the Buddha prefers to characterize the happiness of perfect desirelessness by the standing formula: *Etaṁ santam etam panītam,* "This is peaceful, this is exalted and sublime." "Neither the great ocean, nor the earth nor any mountain range, nor the expanse of the heavens can furnish a likeness of the sublimity of the Master's release."[3]

Let the reader imagine himself on a solitary mountain to which no sound penetrates and from which there is presented a mighty Alpine panorama, a picture of motionlessness and of a breathless silence that soars aloft and vanishes into the air.

1. *Maitrāyaṇī-Upaniṣad,* F. Max Müller's Translation.
2. *Udāna* 11, 2.
3. Psalms of the Monks, v. 1013.

Whoever in such a situation is most deeply affected and becomes oblivious of himself, already has a disposition to true happiness and will not find it difficult to see that, when the Buddha knew himself to be for ever in possession of the Great Peace, not even the most rapturous state of happiness within worldly situations could stir in him the slightest desire. "The Perfectly Awakened One walks on the sacred path, he is blessed by the peace of his mind, has risen above al lthings, has cast off all fetters, and from desiring has attained to desirelessness" (*vanā nibbānam āgatam*) "detached from pleasure as gold is from quartz, he is happy in the state beyond sensual pleasures."[1]

The majesty of the Great Peace in one who goes the way to the Absolute is so sublime that he feels disgust at his own personality and at the whole phenomenal world. "He feels disgust at the eye and at forms . . . at the ear and sounds . . . at the nose and odours . . . at the tongue and juices . . . at the body and objects of touch . . . at the organ of thought and the objects of thought,"[2] till even this disgust sublimates into holy equanimity.

The full significance of such words can be appreciated only by one who experiences them within himself. In this connection the following claim is relevant, although it is often misunderstood: "I have penetrated to this reality (*dhamma*), which is profound, difficult to behold, hard to grasp, peaceful, exalted, not accessible to mere abstract thought, and to be experienced only by the wise." Only the man who experiences complete desirelessness knows what supreme happiness is. Only the man who has experienced inner well-being may enter into a discussion of happiness. Otherwise, he speaks of a matter about which he knows nothing.

The Buddha repeatedly invites the man of goodwill to look beyond sensual pleasures and he will then discern the bliss possible to him in detaching himself from the world, including his own personality. To some extent a man must already be disposed to do this. He must, in fact, be included among the good among those in whom entanglement in their own personality has been loosened to the extent that they feel for the

1. Psalms of the Monks, b. 227.
2. *Majjh. Nik.*, 147th *sutta.*

suffering of others, and so, at the sight of the suffering of others, sympathize or suffer with them. The Buddha has nothing to say to the man who is not yet acquainted with this feeling of compassion and who may even declare such sentiment to be a weakness. But whoever feels compassion for another's suffering already experiences in every act of renunciation he imposes on himself in order to help others the first glimpse of true happiness. This is evinced in the words, "It is more blessed to give than to receive." The man who goes beyond this and, in the knowledge of the pernicious nature of his selfish impulses, consciously takes up the struggle against them and cultivates an active love for his neighbour, will soon experience the blissful feeling of genuine self-contentedness which he has not previously known and which, contrary to the "common man's miry weal", does not lead to disillusionment. His actions are no longer contrary to his innermost being. They are in harmony with it. At the outset he will experience the truth of the words, "Things in space knock against one another." Thus the feeling of self-contentedness can assert itself only in a constant struggle with sensual and selfish tendencies. The more a man practises detachment and the more he extends thoughtfulness to his fellow-beings, the easier does detachment become. Finally he must experience the truth of the claim: "For him who has detached himself from the pleasures of the senses, life becomes a unique day of rest."

At the same time he becomes ever more inclined to pass from the mere study of the *anattā*-idea as the source of all denial of desire to meditation on it. In this way he will perceive intuitively more and more the entire mechanism of his personality as foreign to his Self.[1] In time there appears the "great and gradually felt experience" spoken of in the 118th *sutta* of the *Majjh.-Nik.* We penetrate into the "unnamable, laid hold of in our innermost",[2] and at the same time we enter the first stages of the *Great Peace.* The initial renunciation calls for an expenditure of energy, but ever less effort is required. Renunciation becomes the characteristic quality of an increasing

1. (*Psalms of the Monks*, vv, 1160 ff.).
2. *Dh.*, v. 218.

absense of wants, of desirelessness. Craving becomes impossible, and so does regret. Detachment increases until it is complete. In this way poverty is seen to be the state that is truly adequate. It makes for freedom from care and trouble, and, in consequence, is blissful in the highest degree. "How happily we live, we who possess nothing, we are like the Pure Gods."[1]

Finally, a man may one day see himself at the summit, either in this life or in a later form of existence, where he overflows wih infinite kindness to all that lives, while, at the same time, he is able to see in the entire mechanism of his personality only an ocean of suffering ("whatever is felt appertains to suffering"). For this reason, he faces that suffering as so complete a stranger that every desire, all will, evaporates, and with the Perfectly Awakened One he can say: "The will to become (existence) has been abolished by the sage and fresh becoming . . . having gathered his thoughts full of inward bliss, he shatters his own becoming." His last death results only in his becoming invisible to his fellow-beings: ". . . it is impossible to discover the path of those who are wholly released, have crossed the flood of fettering sensual pleasure, and have (there) found unshakeable well-being."[2] *Peaceful, exalted and sublime is this state, namely the repose of all vital activities, the release from all attributes, the disappearance of the thirsting will, freedom from allurement, the abolition (of perception and sensation), nibbāna* ! Schopenhaur said: "We all have a lasting sentiment or instinctive feeling that . . . . under this reality in which we live and exist, there lies hidden a second and quite different one, which is the thing-in-itself, the (the truly real) to this (our present life's dream)."[3] To this does the Buddhist saint awake.

The reader who has followed us until now will begin to understand the words with which the Buddha frequently characterizes his doctrine of salvation: "It is gladsome in its beginning, gladsome in its continuation, and gladsome in its culmination."

1. *Dh.*, v. 200.
2. *Digh. Nik.* XVI; *Udāna* 8, 10.
3. New Paralipomena S 146.

COMPLETE WORKS OF GEORGE GRIMM

The Doctrine of the Buddha, The Religion of Reason and Meditation.
2. edition—413 pages—DM 20—Akademie-Verlag, Berlin W1, Leipziger Strabe 3-4.

La Religion du Bouddha. La Religion de la Connaissance.

2. Edition—306 pages, Verlag Adrien Maisonneuve, Paris, 11 Rue Saint-Sulpice 6e) Fr. 18.75.

Die Lehre des Buddho, Die Religion der Vernunft und der Meditation.

15-16 thousand—516 pages—Holle-Verlag, Baden-Baden. Neue Sonderausgabe, Preis DM 14.80 (früher DM 34).

Buddhistische Meditationen.

Ein Brevier. 2. edition—396 pages--Baum-Verlag Herm. Bauer KG., 78, Freiburg/Br., Tunibergstr. 7, DM 19, 80.

Das Glück, die Botschaft des Buddha.

4. edition, Baum-Verlag Herm. Bauer KG., 78 Freiburg/Br., Tunibergstr. 7, DM 12.80.

Der Samsāro, die Weltenirrfahrt der Wesen.

2. edition—188 pages—Heinrich Schwab-Verlag, 786 Schopfheim/Baden, DM 12.50.

Buddhistische Weisheit.

4. edition — 128 pages — Heinrich Schwab-Verlag, 786. Schopfheim/Baden, DM 12.50.

Der Buddhaweg für Dich.

248 pages—with a picture of author—Baum-Verlag Herm. Bauer KG., 78 Freiburg/Br., Tunibergstr. 7, DM 9, 80.

Die Botschaft des Buddha der Schlüssel zur Unsterblichkeit.

85 pages—Baum-Verlag Herm. Bauer KG., 78 Freiburg/Br., Tunibergstr. 7, DM 3.80.

Ewige Fragen.

Die religiosen Grundprobleme and there Losung im indischen Geiste.

3. edition—83 pages—Otto-Wilhelm-Barth-Verlag, Weilheim/Obb., DM 5, 80.

P. J. SAHER

Eastern Wisdom and Western Thought.
George Allen & Unwin, London 1969.
Happinese and Immortality.
George Grimm's Investigations into the Secrets of Buddhism.
George Allen and Unwin, Price net 40 s=£2.00

Edited by P. J. Saher :

M. Keller—Grimm and Annagarika Dhammapāla Im Lichte des Meisters. Die Lehre des Buddha in Frage und Antwort.
Aloys Henn-Verlag, 1971.

materials of the outer world, is the supporter of the other component, namely vitality, called also *nāma* or *nāmakāya*, mental body. The latter constitutes a *quality* of the material body, in the same way that magnetism constitutes a quality of iron. As magnetism makes iron magnetic, vitality renders the material body organic. That is, it changes inorganic matter into organic matter.

Only the latter, in the form of a corporeal organism, is capable of arousing consciousness and thereby of bringing about contact with the outer world. As the Buddha said, "... both are inextricably connected; only as a unity may they come into existence."

From these expositions results the insight that eye-consciousness, ear-consciousness, etc., do not arise in the brain, as is inferred from the fact that, if a nerve leading from an organ of sense to the brain is severed, nothing more is seen or heard, etc. Eye-consciousness, ear-consciousness, etc., arise immediately in the eye, the ear, etc. The severing of the nerve merely interrupts contact with the source of the current, so that the nerve, so to speak, is no longer charged with vitality.

Thus the bodily organism as the six-sense-machine and as the substratum of personality, is fully comprehended. But the personality has the further substratum of consciousness. For the possibility of coming into contact with the world depends not only on the bodily organism, but also on this organism arousing consciousness in its sixfold sensual activity. Personality is, in fact, the homogeneous result of the bodily organism and the element of consciousness.

Cognition becomes active only through the interlocking [illegible]

[illegible]

Birth, [illegible] the first [illegible] fundamental cause craving, "and all grasping is rooted in thirst, in willing [illegible] the search for the cause of our ever repeated

BIBLIOGRAPHY

AL-GHAZZALI. *Confessions*. Translated by Claud Field (London, 1909).

ANSARI OF HERAT. *The Invocations of Sheikh Abdullah Ansari of Herat*. Translated by Sardar Sir Jogendra Singh (London, 1939).

ATTAR. *Selections*. Translated by Margaret Smith (London, 1932).

AUGUSTINE, ST. *Confessions*. (numerous editions).

AUROBINDO, SRI. *The Life Divine*, 3 vols. (Calcutta, 1939).

BAKER, AUGUSTINE. *Holy Wisdom* (London, 1876).

BEAUSOBRE, JULIA DE. *The Woman Who Could Not Die* (London and New York, 1938).

BERNARD OF CLAIRVAUX, ST. *The Steps of Humility* (Cambridge, Mass., 1940).

On the Love of God (New York, 1937).

Selected Letters (London, 1904). An admirably lucid account of St. Bernard's thought may be found in *The Mystical Doctrine of Saint Bernard*, by Professor Etienne Gilson (London and New York, 1940).

BERTOCCI, PETER A. *The Empirical Argument for God in Late British Philosophy* (Cambridge, Mass., 1938).

Bhagavad-Gītā. Among many translations of this Hindu scripture the best, from a literary point of view, is that of Swami Prabhavananda and Christopher Isherwood (Los Angeles, 1944). Valuable notes, based upon the commentaries of Śaṅkara, are to be found in Swami Nikhilananda's edition (New York, 1944), and Professor Franklin Edgerton's literal translation (Cambridge, Mass., 1944) is preceded by a long and scholarly introduction.

BINYON, L. *The Flight of the Dragon* (London, 1911).

BOEHME, JAKOB. Some good introduction is needed to the work of this important but difficult mystic. On the theological and devotional side the Danish Bishop H.L.

Martensen's *Jacob Boehmi* (trans., London, 1885) is recommended; or from a more philosophical viewpoint A. Koyre's splendid volume *La Philosophie de Jacob Boehme* (not yet translated. Paris, 1929) or H. H. Brinton's *The Mystic Will* (New York, 1930).

BRAHMANANDA, SWAMI. Records of his teaching and a biography by Swami Prabhavananda are contained in *The Eternal Companion* (Los Angeles, 1944).

CAMUS, JEAN PIERRE. *The Spirit of St. Francois de Sales* London n.d).

CAUSSADE, J.P. DE. *Abandonment* (New York, 1887).

Spiritual Letters, 3 vols. (London, 1937).

CHANTAL, ST. JEANNE FRANCOISE. *Selected Letters* (London and New York, 1918).

CHAPMAN, ABBOT JOHN. *Spiritual Letters* (London, 1935).

CHUANG TZU. *Chuang Tzu, Mystic, Moralist and Social Reformer.* Translated by Herbert Giles (Shanghai, 1936).

Musings of a Chinese Mystic (London, 1920).

Chinese Philosophy in Classical Times. Translated by E.R. Hughes (London, 1943).

The Cloud of Unknowing (with commentary by Augustine Baker). Edited with an introduction by Justice McCann (London, 1924).

COOMARASWAMY, ANANDA K. *Buddha and the Gospel of Buddhism* (New York, 1916).

The Transformation of Nature in Art (Cambridge, Mass., 1935).

Hinduism and Buddhism (New York, n.d.).

CURTIS, A.M. *The Way of Silence* (Burton Bradstock. Dorset, 1937).

DEUSSEN, PAUL. *The Philosophy of the Upanishads* (London, 1906).

DIONYSIUS THE AREOPAGITE. *On the Divine Names and the Mystical Theology.* Translated with an introduction by C.E. Rolt (London, 1920).

ECKHART, MEISTER. *Works*, translated by C.B. Evans (London, 1924).

Meister Eckhart, A Modern Translation. By R. B. Blakney (New York, 1941).

EVANS-WENTZ, W.Y. *The Tibetan Book of the Dead* (New York, 1927).

Tibet's Great Yogi, Milarepa (New York. 1928).

Tibetan Yoga and Secret Doctrines (New York, 1935).

The Following of Christ. Unknown author, but mistakenly attributed to Tauler in the first English edition (London 1886).

FOX, GEORGE. *Journal* (London, 1911).

FROST BEDE. *The Art of Mental Prayer* (London, 1940).

Saint John of the Cross (London 1937).

GARRIGOU-LAGRANGE, R. *Christian Perfection and Contemplation* (London and St. Louis, 1937).

GODDARD, DWIGHT. *A Buddhist Bible* (published by the editor Thetford, Maine, 1938). This volume contains translations of several Mahāyāna texts not to be found, or to be found only with much difficulty, elsewhere. Among these are 'The Diamond Sūtra,' 'The Suraṅgama Sūtra,' 'The Laṅkāvatāra Sūtra,' 'The Awakening of Faith' and 'The Sūtra of the Sixth Patriarch.'

GUENON, RENE. *Man and His Becoming according to the Vedānta* (London, n.d.).

East and West (London, 1941).

The Crisis of the Modern World (London, 1942).

HEARD, GERALD. *The Creed of Christ* (New York, 1940).

The Code of Christ (New York, 1941).

Preface to Prayer (New York, 1944).

HILTON, WALTER. *The Scale of Perfection* (London, 1927).

HUEGEL, FRIEDRICH VON. *The Mystical Element in Religion as Studied in Saint Catherine of Genoa and Her Friends* (London. 1923).

IBN TUFAIL. *The Awakening of the Soul.* Translated by Paul Bronnle (London, 1910).

The Imitation of Christ. Whitford's translation, edited by E.J. Klein (New York, 1941).

INGE, W.R. *Christian Mysticism* (London, 1899).

Studies of English Mystics—including William Law (London, 1906).

JOHN OF THE CROSS, ST. *Works*, 3 vols. (London, 1934-1935).

JONES, RUFUS. *Studies in Mystical Religion.*

The Spiritual Reformers in the 16th and 17th Centuries (New York, 1914).

The Flowering of Mysticism (New York, 1939).

JORGENSEN, JOHANNES. *Saint Catherine of Siena* (London, 1938).

JULIANA OF NORWICH. *Revelations of Divine Love*(London, 1917).

LAO TZU. There are many translations of the Tao Teh King. Consult and compare those of Arthur Waley in *The Way and Its Power* (London, 1933), ofF. R. Hughes in *Chinese Philosophy in Classical Times* (Everyman's Library) and of Ch'u Ta-Kao (London, 1927) reprinted in *The Bible of the World* (New York, 1939).

LAW, WILLIAM. Several modern editions of his *Serious Call* are available. But none of Law's still finer and much more distinctly mystical works, such as *The Spirit of Prayer* and *The Spirit of Love,* have been reprinted in full in recent years. Long extracts from them may however be found in Stephen Hobhouse's *Selected Mystical Writings of William Law* (London, 1939) (a work which also contains some useful 'Notes and Studies in the mystical theology of William Law and Jacob Boehme') and in the same writer's *William Law and Eighteenth Century Quakerism* (London, 1927). Alexander Whyte also compiled a fine anthology, *Characters and Characteristics of William Law* (4th ed. London, 1907; while for the student there is Christopher Walton's extra-ordinary encyclopaedic collection of *Notes and Materials for an adequate biography of William Law* (London, 1856).

LEEN EDWARD, *Progress through Mental Prayer* (London, 1940).

McKEON, RICHARD. Selections from Medieval Philossophers, 2 vols. (New York, 1929).

The Mirror of Simple Souls. Author unknown (London, 1927).

NICHOLAS OF CUSA. *The Idiot* (San Francisco, 1940).

The Vision of God (London and New York, 1928).

NICHOLSON, R. *The Mystics of Islam* (London, 1914).

OMAN, JOHN. *The Natural and the Supernatural* (London, 1938).

OTTO, RUDOLF. *India's Religion of Grace* (London, 1930).

Mysticism East and West (London, 1932).

PATANJALI. *Yoga Aphorisms.* Translated with a commentary by Swami Vivekananda (New York, 1899).

PLOTINUS. *The Essence of Plotinus* (G. H. Turnbull, New York, 1934). A good anthology of this very important and voluminous mystic.

PONNELLE, L. and L. BORDET. *St. Philip Neri and the Roman Society of His Time* (London, 1932).

POULAIN, A. *The Graces of Interior Prayer* (London, 1910).

POURRAT, P. *Christian Spirituality*, 3 vols. (London, 1922).

PRATT, J.B. *The Pilgrimage of Buddhism* (New York, 1928).

RADHAKRISHNAN, S. *The Hindu View of Life* (London and New York, 1927).

Indian Philosophy (London and New York, 1923-1927).

Eastern Religions and Western Thought (New York, 1939).

The Dhammapada, London 1950.

RAMAKRISHNA SRI. *The Gospel of Sri Ramakrishna.* Translated from the Bengali narrative of 'M' by Swami Nikhilananda (New York, 1942).

RUMI-JALAL-UDDIN. *Masnavi* Translated by E. H. Whinfield (London, 1898).

RUYSBROECK, JAN VAN. *The Adornment of the Spiritual Marriage* (London, 1916). Consult also the studies by Evelyn Underhill (London, 1915) and Wautier d'Aygalliers (London, 1925).

SALES, ST. FRANÇOIS DE. *Introduction to the Devout Life* (numerous editions).

Treatise on the Love of God (new edition, Westminster, Md., 1942).

Spiritual Conferences (London, 1868).

see also J.P. Camus.

The Secret of the Golden Flower. Translated from the Chinese by Richard Wilhelm. Commentary by Dr. C. G. Jung (London and New York, 1931).

SPURGEON, CAROLINE. *Mysticism in English Literature* (Cambridge, 1913).

STOCKS, J.L. *Time, Cause and Eternity* (London, 1938).

STOUT, G. F. *Mind and Matter* (London, 1931).

Sūtra Spoken by the Sixth Patriarch, Hui Neng. Translated by

Wung Mou-lam (Shanghai, 1930). Reprinted in *A Buddhist Bible* (Thetford, 1938).

SUZUKI, B. L. *Mahāyāna Buddhism* (London, 1938).

SUZUKI, D. T, *Studies in Zen Buddhism* (London, 1927).

Studies in the Laṅkāvatāra Sūtra (Kyoto and London, 1935).

Manual of Zen Buddhism (Kyota, 1935).

TAGORE RABINDRANATH. *One Hundred Poems of Kabir* (London, 1915).

TAULER, JOHANN. *Life and Sermons* (London, 1907).

The Inner Way (London, 1909).

Consult Inge's *Christian Mysticism,* Rufus Jones's *Studies in Mystical Religion* and Pourat's *Christian Spirituality.*

TENNANT, F.R. *Philosophical Theology* (Cambridge, 1923).

Theologia Germanica. Winkworth's translation (new edition, London, 1937).

TILLYARD, AELFRIDA. *Spiritual Exercises* (London, 1927).

TRAHERNE, THOMAS. *Centuries of Meditation* (London, 1908).

Consult *Thomas Traharne, A Critical Biography,* by Gladys I. Wade (Princeton, 1944).

UNDERHILL, EVELYN. *Mysticism* (London, 1924).

The Mystics of the Church (London, 1925).

UPANIṢADS. *The Thirteen Principal Upaniṣads.* Translated by R.E. Hume (New York, 1931).

The ten Principal Upaniṣads. Translated by Shree Purohit and W.B. Yeats (London, 1937).

The Himalayas of the Soul. Translated by J. Mascaro (London, 1938).

WATTS, ALAN W. *The Spirit of Zen* (London, 1936).

WHITNEY, JANET. *John Woolman, American Quaker* (Boston, 1942).

INDEX